Labor Relations Law
in State
and Local Government

Labor Relations Law in State and Local Government

David A. Dilts, Clarence R. Deitsch, and Ali Rassuli

Q

Quorum Books
Westport, Connecticut • London

Library of Congress Cataloging-in-Publication Data

Dilts, David A.
　　Labor relations law in state and local government / David A.
　　Dilts, Clarence R. Deitsch, and Ali Rassuli.
　　　　p.　cm.
　　Includes bibliographical references and index.
　　ISBN 0–89930–414–1 (alk. paper)
　　1. State governments—United States—Officials and employees.
　　2. Collective labor agreements—Local officials and employees—
　　United States.　I. Deitsch, Clarence R.　II. Rassuli, Ali.
　　III. Title.
　　KF5390.D55　1992
　　344.73′01890413539—dc20
　　[347.3041890413539]　　　92–8405

British Library Cataloguing in Publication Data is available.

Library of Congress Catalog Card Number: 92–8405
ISBN: 0–89930–414–1

First published in 1992

Quorum Books, 88 Post Road West, Westport, CT 06881
An imprint of Greenwood Publishing Group, Inc.

Printed in the United States of America

The paper used in this book complies with the
Permanent Paper Standard issued by the National
Information Standards Organization (Z39.48–1984).

10　9　8　7　6　5　4　3　2　1

Contents

Preface   vii

I. Introduction

   1. Introduction to Public Sector Labor Law   3

   2. An Introduction to Labor Law and Collective
       Bargaining in the Public Sector   13

   3. The Public Sector and Collective Bargaining   37

II. The Law

   4. Administrative Law Agencies and Their
       Functions   51

   5. Unionization, Organization, and Employee–
       Employer Rights   63

   6. The Law and Negotiations   81

   7. Impasse Procedures   99

   8. The Effects of Law on Collective Bargaining 111

   9. Bargaining During the Life of the Contract   127

10. Public Sector Labor Law: Conclusions, Trends,
and Possibilities   139

Appendix: Public Employment Relations Board Rules
and Regulations of the Iowa Code   147

Annotated Bibliography   181

Index   193

Preface

Labor law in the public sector is different from that found in the private sector. In the private sector there are only two major bodies of law that apply: the Railway Labor Act, which applies to the nation's railroads and airlines, and the Taft-Hartley Act, which applies to the remainder of the private sector that has a substantial effect on interstate commerce. The presentation and analysis of private sector labor law is therefore relatively easy.

Federal sector labor law has grown out of several executive orders. Congress passed the 1978 Civil Service Reform Act to replace the federal executive orders and establish statutory enabling law. The labor law in the federal sector recognizes a significant body of federal statutes, rules, and regulations, thereby making the legal landscape more complex than private sector law.

Labor law governing labor–management relations for state and local government is far different from either private or federal sector labor laws. Each state is responsible for its own public policy towards public employee unions. To date, more than four dozen state labor laws are in force. There are also dozens of city and local ordinances governing labor management relations. To further complicate the scene, most of these statutes and ordinances incorporate or recognize external law as binding in governing labor-management relations. This complicated tangle of law has discouraged analysis and presentation. The purpose of this book is to present a unified and useful analysis of the labor law found at the state and local level.

There are several persons who deserve recognition for their contributions to this project. Naturally, our wives and children have sacrificed time so that the research could be accomplished and the manuscript prepared. Our indebtedness is acknowledged and will be repaid.

We also wish to thank our editors, Eric Valentine and Meg Fergusson, for their patience and support. Fred Witney provided a great deal of inspiration, and Bill Walsh gave many helpful contributions. To these four go our undying gratitude.

I

Introduction

1

Introduction to Public Sector Labor Law

This chapter provides a brief discussion of what the authors intend to accomplish with this text, a plan of the book, and brief introductory discussions of employee–employer relations and labor law in the public sector. The plan of the book offers a preview of the topics to be covered. The discussion of public sector employer–employee relations is intended to develop a basic understanding of why unionization and collective bargaining in the public sector are such controversial topics. Discussion of why unions were late bloomers in the public sector also provides some insights into the nature of public sector collective bargaining as well as its environment.

Public sector collective bargaining is one of the few areas in which unions can still claim some degree of growth. Much has been written concerning labor relations and collective bargaining in the private sector. There is also a wealth of published knowledge concerning labor law in the private sector. There is, however, a slim but growing literature concerning labor relations in the public sector. Very little has been written on public sector labor law, and what little there is has focused on the Civil Service Reform Act of 1978 dealing with federal employees. In the case of state and local government, the variety of statutes has limited the general applicability of law and thus has discouraged writers working in this area.

The National Labor Relations Act specifically excludes governmental employers from coverage.[1] The Civil Service Reform Act of 1978 applies only to federal employees.[2] Therefore, if the collective bargaining rights of state and local government employees are to be protected, each jurisdiction, for example, the state, must enact its own labor law.

This book is written with both practitioners and academics in mind. It will offer a full range of topical coverage of public sector law. Because of the numerous state and local statutes it is impossible to provide a detailed analysis of each statute. Where possible, generalizations will be offered, where not possible, comparisons will be drawn concerning the variety of ways jurisdictions have dealt with specific legal issues.

Two of the authors are professional arbitrators and fact finders; the third is a labor economist. The authors are neither pro-union nor pro-management, but are neutral. That does not mean the book will be free of the authors' own views on how the world works; it simply means that one should not expect the authors to side with either labor or management in the presentations contained herein.

PUBLIC SECTOR BARGAINING AND LABOR LAW

The public sector includes many levels of government and a large array of occupations. The focal point of this book are the state and local governmental levels. There are differences in collective bargaining at the federal and state levels, but for the most part these differences revolve around the sizes of the respective agencies and the nature of the legal environment. Some of what is examined here is fully applicable to the federal sector but is packaged to be most useful to those interested in such state and local governmental employees as firefighters, police officers, teachers, state highway employees, and the agencies in which they work.

It is the negotiators operating in the public sector who have been largely ignored by authors of labor relations and labor law texts. At best, a chapter may be found that gives a general overview of the public sector or discusses a specific, often technical point in either the labor law or collective bargaining, but these single-chapter treatments offer little in the way of practical and useful information in preparing for labor disputes, organizations, or contract negotiations.[3]

With the exception of a few articles in academic literature and even fewer in trade literature, little has been written concerning the labor law the public sector.

OUTLINE OF THE BOOK

This book is divided into two major parts: Part I provides an introduction to public sector labor law, and Part II offers an in-depth analysis of specific legal issues important to collective bargaining in the public sector.

Chapter 1 is devoted to a brief overview of state collective bargaining statutes. It examines why it was left to the states to enact their own collective bargaining laws and makes comparisons among the various states concerning the coverage of those statutes. It introduces election policies, scope of bargaining, employee rights, unfair labor practice provisions, and other portions of the various statutory schemes important to an understanding of collective bargaining.

The current status of public sector labor law is introduced in Chapter 2. This chapter examines the extent of state labor law and the basic structure of these statutes. Chapter 3 focuses on collective bargaining in the public sector and why labor law is a patchwork of statutes applicable only to specific state or local jurisdictions. It examines the unique characteristics of public employers and their impact on both the labor law and collective bargaining that have evolved in state and local government.

Part I is the foundation upon which the discussion of the specific elements of the public sector labor law is built. Part II begins with Chapter 4, an analysis of the structure and operation of the various administrative law agencies charged with the responsibility of enforcement of the jurisdiction's labor law. Applicable unfair labor practice provisions will also be examined in this chapter.

Chapter 5 is a discussion of employer, employee, and union rights; the law governing union organization and certification procedures. Specific examinations of the assignment of rights to the various principles is followed with an analysis of the certification process and its variants.

Chapter 6 concerns contract negotiations. The various legal requirements concerning the scope of bargaining are examined. The duty to negotiate and unfair labor practice provisions concerning bargaining activities are also examined in this chapter.

Chapter 7 is a detailed discussion of the law concerning impasse procedures. The enabling statutes concerning mediation, fact finding, and interest arbitration are examined, as are enforcement and the scope of neutral authority.

Chapter 8 examines the effects of statutory impasse procedures on collective bargaining. Attention is turned to the long-run effects of impasse resolution procedures on the nature and conduct of the parties' collective bargaining relations.

Chapter 9 examines the duty to bargain during the life of the collective bargaining agreement. Topics presented include grievances, grievance arbitration, and modification or repudiation of a negotiated contract.

Chapter 10, the last chapter, presents conclusions concerning the current status of labor law concerning state and local labor law.

The appendix offers an example of a state collective bargaining law followed by an annotated bibliography of books and articles concerning public sector labor law.

EMPLOYEE–EMPLOYER RELATIONS IN THE PUBLIC SECTOR

The growth of the public sector has been rather steady over recent U.S. history. One out of every five employed persons in the United States works for either federal, state, or local governments.[4] The importance of the public sector as a major source of jobs, hence income, should be obvious from this fact alone. The public sector is also of prime importance in the U.S. economic system because of the idea of public goods. There is often a distinction made between public and private goods. Private goods are those that can be distributed to a single end-producer who can reserve their consumption to himself or herself exclusively. These goods have a value to the specific person who is willing to pay for them since the consumption cannot be had any other way. Economists typically use the examples of beer and pizza, and both of these are good examples of private goods. A public good differs in that the end consumer cannot necessarily provide the service without participation by others and frequently cannot preclude others from its consumption even if able to provide it to himself or herself. National defense, highways, and schools are examples of public goods. A highway, school, or army are very expensive propositions, and it is doubtful that any single consumer could provide those goods for himself or herself. A school is a good that can be duplicated in the private sector, but only by those with sufficient incomes or wealth to pay for its services. Schools become a public good in most respects because the education of the general population provides basic and marketable skills for those who could not otherwise provide themselves with such educations, so it's better to educate than to provide public welfare or simply allow starvation to rid society of those unable to afford schooling.

A highway, once it is built, is difficult to patrol and therefore to deny access to one's neighbors. Turnpike authorities have been successful in building, maintaining, and charging for the services of highways, but generally only through the public sector. National defense falls under this category. Since all of society benefits from national defense and transportation and no single person is easily excluded from the system, they become public goods.

The requirement to provide public goods requires government. Government, to function properly, requires employees with various skills. Employees require incomes to maintain themselves and their households. The government then exchanges compensation for services rendered, and taxpayers exchange tax dollars for services provided by government. This is a simple flow of goods and services, except that one portion of it involves government and its ability to tax. The American public has always been suspicious of this because of a perceived lack of motivation by elected officials to properly control government and the general apathy of the voting public. Government and its role are therefore highly controversial topics and have been so throughout U.S. history.[5] These components can be thought of as roughly defining the economic environment of public sector collective bargaining. The power to tax combined with the necessity of providing public goods and with an economic history of suspicion of government provide the general framework for the economic environment. These issues will be discussed in greater detail in Chapter 3.

Labor unions have not always enjoyed popularity in this country; even today they are viewed with a great deal of suspicion from certain quarters. In early U.S. history, unions were regarded as criminal conspiracies per se because their objective was to raise wages and improve conditions for the working classes. This was regarded by many, including the courts, as theft, because if more was spent on labor, then someone would have to pay a higher price for goods and services, and workers ought not be allowed to band together for the purposes of theft.[6] In the first of these court cases shoemakers (private sector employees, not public) were found guilty of a criminal conspiracy because they formed a union to prevent wage cutting. The lot and public image of labor unions improved only slightly over the next 125 years, so this country has a long history of little regard for collective bargaining or unions.[7]

It cannot be any wonder to anyone why labor relations and collective bargaining in the public sector are such controversial topics. The wedding of two extremely controversial and visible institutions could not help but provide for public debate and skepticism. What is maybe more astounding is that public sector collective bargaining has been as widely adopted and successful a system of employee–employer relations as it has over the past few decades.

For decades prior to the advent of the widespread unionization of the public sector, traditional organizing attempts met with failure. This was especially true during the 1930s and 1940s, the boom period for industrial unions. Several reasons have been offered for this difficulty in organizing public employees. Public employment offered benefits not found in the private sector; "merit hiring, broad fringe benefits, almost absolute job security, and an assured income (not dependent on vagaries of weather, availability of risk capital, or the ebb and flow of fads and fashion)" more than offset any of the claimed benefits from unionization.[8] "In truth, these were the trade-offs for private-sector unionism."[9]

As these public-employment benefits declined during the post-war 1950s and the benefits and compensation associated with private sector employment overtook the public sector, then public employees became more inclined to organizing and collective bargaining. Public employers by the 1970s were far behind private sector employees in compensation and were beginning to find that job security and most of the other amenities associated with public employment had disappeared; unions were the only way to prevent further erosion and possibly the reclamation of lost benefits.[10]

This discussion illustrates why employee–employer relations and especially collective bargaining in the public sector has been so controversial. This sociopolitical environment of public sector collective bargaining has provided one significant obstacle to the evolution of mature collective bargaining in this arena. The sociopolitical aspects of the environment are those public opinions developed over the years concerning the role of government and organized labor. The deep-seated beliefs that public sector employees have had it too easy for too long and that their managers have been too altruistic are important facets of this environment. This discussion also clearly demonstrates that collective bargaining in the public sector is a much newer phenomenon than its counterpart in the private sector. The public sector is maturing rapidly and may be the mainstay of the U.S. economy and maybe even of organized labor into the twenty-first century, but only if there are continued increases in the sophistication and competence of the parties to public sector collective bargaining and the neutrals who serve them in their impasse-resolution endeavors. The increases in both the efficiency and fairness of government operation that good labor-management relations can provide can improve the lot of all Americans. This is another very good, if not more idealistic, reason to embark on this book.

SUMMARY AND CONCLUSIONS

This book is written for practitioners and academics in the field of public sector labor relations. While the labor law is similar in many cases to that found in the private or federal sectors, there are often significant differences; these will be presented in the following chapters.

The necessity to provide public goods together with the government's ability to tax provide much of the economic environment of collective bargaining. The historic suspicion directed at government and unions in this country adds much to the sociopolitical environment of public sector collective bargaining.

The relatively late organization of unions in the public sector was due primarily to the generally good working conditions, compensation, and job security of public sector jobs. As these characteristics of public employment eroded, so did public employee resistance to unionization and collective bargaining.

NOTES

1. Section 2, Labor Management Relations Act of 1947 (Taft-Hartley), 61 Stat. 136.

2. 5 U.S.C. 71.

3. For example, see Benjamin J. Taylor and Fred Witney, *Labor Relations Law*, 4th ed. (Englewood Cliffs, N.J.: Prentice-Hall, 1983), Chapter 21; David A. Dilts and Clarence R. Deitsch, *Labor Relations* (New York: Macmillan, 1983), Chapter 15; Frank Elkouri and Edna A. Elkouri, *How Arbitration Works*, 4th ed. (Washington, D.C.: Bureau of National Affairs, 1985), Chapter 18; and John A. Fossum, *Labor Relations: Development, Structure, Process*, 3d ed. (Plano, Tex.: Business Publications, 1985), Chapter 15.

4. Alan E. Bent and T. Zane Reeves, *Collective Bargaining in the Public Sector* (Menlo Park, Calif.: Benjamin/Cummings, 1978), 3.

5. See Milton Friedman, *Capitalism & Freedom* (Chicago: University of Chicago Press, 1962), for a reasoned conservative and suspicious view of government.

6. Commonwealth v. Pullis (1806).

7. An interesting history of the American labor movement is to be found in Harold C. Livesay, *Samuel Gompers and Organized Labor in America* (Boston: Little, Brown and Company, 1978).

8. Sam Zagoria, editor, *Public Workers and Public Unions.* (Englewood Cliffs, N.J.: Prentice-Hall, Inc., Spectrum Books, 1972), 1.

9. Ibid.

10. Ibid.

2

An Introduction to Labor Law and Collective Bargaining in the Public Sector

The need for government in these respects arises because absolute freedom is impossible. However attractive anarchy may be as a philosophy, it is not feasible in a world of imperfect men. Men's freedoms can conflict, and when they do, one man's freedom must be limited to preserve another's—as a Supreme Court Justice once put it, "My freedom to move my fist must be limited by the proximity of your chin."
—Milton Friedman, *Government in a Free Society*

This chapter is an introduction to labor law in the public sector. Labor law is a dynamic collection of statutory regulations. Each jurisdiction is free to regulate labor–management relations within its own borders as it sees fit. This has resulted in significant differences among states, even though there are several generalizations that can be made. Before proceeding to discussions about specific aspects of the law, the limits must be identified. That is the purpose of this chapter.

The first section of this chapter introduces the reader to the role of labor law in employer–employee relations in the public sector. The remainder of the chapter is devoted to introducing the basic provisions typically found in the labor laws of the various states. Detailed analyses of the major provisions of state statutes are reserved for their respective chapters.

AN INTRODUCTION TO PUBLIC SECTOR LABOR LAW

Public sector labor law is complicated and controversial. Proponents of public sector unionism argue that protective legislation is a prerequisite to democracy. Without an independent labor movement there would be no democracy in the workplace, and political democracy may even be threatened. Opponents, on the other hand, contend that public employees are treated better than are private sector employees and are servants of the taxpaying public, and therefore cannot be permitted to have the same rights as private sector employees. The public sector legal landscape is a product of the controversy.

The term *labor law* has been used to describe the body of statutory and case law that governs the total array of employer–employee relations. This could, potentially, include everything from regulation of pension funds to the doctrine of employment-at-will. For present purposes a much narrower definition of labor law is desirable in that the purpose of this examination is to provide a basis for understanding the legal environment of collective bargaining in state and local government.

In the broadest sense, labor law refers to those laws that govern the various aspects of employee–employer relations. This implies a diverse collection of law with a wide variety of focal points. This broadest definition includes such items as the Civil Rights Act of 1964, the Fair Labor Standards Act, various industrial health and safety statutes, and the Social Security Act as well as those statutes that specifically concern collective bargaining, employees' rights to unionization, and the relation between unions and employers. For present purposes, only the latter is considered the relevant portion of the labor law. In this book labor law will refer only to those statutes that govern the collective bargaining aspects of employer–employee relations in the public sector.

A few remarks are in order concerning the remainder of the law that governs such things as wages, hours, discrimination, and health and safety. The regulatory environment has imposed many employment standards on both the private and the public sector. Many of these standards were at one time subject to collective bargaining, at least in the private sector. Once established by statute, these standards were no longer typically critical issues of negotiations. The recent changes in the coverage of the Fair Labor Standards Act have demonstrated both the dynamic nature of the regulatory environment and how it may influence the public sector. Employer rights to manage a public agency can be modified in several ways. Among the ways these managerial rights can be affected is through statutory intervention, court rulings, and collective bargaining. Those rights bestowed on employees by statutory regulation or court decision are typically not the subject of collective bargaining. For example, the coverage of the Fair Labor Standards Act or an affirmative action program cannot be disturbed or displaced by a collective bargaining agreement returning those rights to management. In this manner the scope, or range, of bargaining issues is limited by actions to regulate the labor market in such a manner as to generate rights for employees.

It is interesting to note that once fixed by statute, employees may gain rights. Organized labor has often pressed for regulatory statutes concerning civil rights, wages, health, and safety as well as other issues. By gaining these rights through statutes, unions believe they are gaining through another forum what may not have been possible to gain through negotiations. There is merit to this position. However, there is a downside to this approach. As employees gain rights through legislative action, rights that may have been obtained at the bargaining table, unions may be reducing their utility to their membership. The regulatory environment outside collective bargaining laws therefore substantially impacts collective bargaining and unions. This impact, however, is not directly caused through collective bargaining and is not analyzed further in this text.

In the public sector the regulatory environment also retains to management's discretion rights that cannot be bargained away. For example, some states have tenure or due-process statutes that retain for management certain decision-making authority concerning the evaluation and tenuring of public school teachers. Unions are effectively barred by many of these statutes from attempting to wrestle those rights away from management.

Whether one accepts the regulatory environment as appropriate or not, the various regulatory laws do affect the nature of public sector collective bargaining. The collective bargaining statutes themselves will frame the respective parties' rights and establish what issues are subject to collective bargaining, but this establishment of rights is typically subject to the provision that the state's constitution or some intervening statute does not preclude bargaining on the topic. This body of law conclusively demonstrates that collective bargaining does not occur in a vacuum, and to understand collective bargaining one must first understand its environment. Labor law provides one important aspect of that environment.

THE FEDERAL AND STATE COLLECTIVE BARGAINING STATUTES

Labor law is a collection of rules that requires and/or prohibits certain activities by both labor and management. The labor law of the United States was enacted by Congress in 1935 because of the perceived need to protect workers' rights to form labor organizations for the purpose of providing relatively unfettered representation of workers' views to their employers. The original labor law was then amended in 1947 to limit certain union activities that were deemed not to be consistent with the intended public policy framed in the original statute. Federal labor law contained a provision that was extremely important in the history and evolution of the labor law governing state and local government employees.[1] This provision is Section 2 (2) of the Taft-Hartley Act, which states in pertinent part:

(2) The term "employer" includes any person acting as an agent of an employer, directly or indirectly, but shall not include . . . any State or political subdivision thereof.

If collective bargaining rights for public employees were to be protected by statute, such protections must be enacted by each state or local legislative branch. The clear language of the Taft-Hartley Act precludes coverage to public employers and their employees. That does not mean employers and employees cannot enter into a collective bargaining arrangement. All it means is that there are no unfair labor practices, administrative law agency, certification, or enforcement procedures upon which the parties may rely.

The result of this language contained in the Taft-Hartley Act is that there is no law of national scope that governs public sector collective bargaining. The adoption of collective bargaining statutes is left to individual jurisdictions. This poses some interesting questions. The public policy of the United States is that there shall not be uniform and consistent treatment of public employers and their employees with regard to collective bargaining. It would appear that some degree of consistency of treatment of all U.S. citizens would be a desirable public policy. In certain states, employees have a right to form and join labor organizations, but no right to bargain collectively; in others public employees have the right not only to bargain collectively but also to strike if no agreement can be reached with the public employer. Such differences have implications not only for public employees but also for managers of public agencies as well as taxpayers and the general public. With a highly mobile society and the proximity of various jurisdictions it is no wonder that this issue has taken on some importance.

It is also interesting to note that there is a disparity between the public and the private sector. Employees in the private sector can expect to have essentially the same collective bargaining rights anywhere they work in the United States. This is certainly not true of public employees. Public employees sometimes enjoin collective bargaining rights that are equivalent to those workers in the private sector, but for the most part they do not. One thing is certain: persons who work in the public sector will find that their rights will vary substantially from one state to another.

There is something to be said for the manner in which Congress decided to handle the public sector with respect to the Taft-Hartley Act. Congress intended that there should be local determination concerning public sector collective bargaining laws. Each state was free to determine what its own public policy should be with respect to the unionization of and bargaining with public employees. This self-determination and local governance is valued by many persons in this country and is not to be taken lightly.

There is another side to this self-determination issue. The various states are the employers of many workers who would seek unionization and collective bargaining rights. It seems oddly inconsistent to many observers that the employer, even though through the legislative branch, can fix the extent and nature of bargaining rights for its own employees. This has lead to the conclusion by some observers and unions that the system of self-determination is inherently unfair to state and local government employees. There are certain jurisdictions where such criticisms seem to be valid; on the other hand, there are jurisdictions that have enacted employees' bargaining rights that are beyond suspicion.

These issues are controversial and worthy of thought, but the real purpose of this chapter is to examine the role that labor law plays in public sector collective bargaining in this country. The lack of consistency in public sector labor law and how public sector bargaining laws have evolved in the United States is in large measure attributable to the public sector's exclusion from Taft-Hartley coverage. This exclusion says much about the perceived role of government and public policy towards public sector negotiations.[2]

PUBLIC SECTOR STATUTES—IN GENERAL

There is substantial variation in the organizational and bargaining rights bestowed on public employees and their unions by law. Some states have enacted statutes that are consistent with and strikingly similar to the Taft-Hartley Act, while others have prohibited public employers from negotiating or entering into collective bargaining agreements with labor unions.[3] For example, there are three states that prohibit school boards from entering into collective bargaining contracts or labor agreements with teacher unions.[4] There are presently thirty-five states that have some form of statute that grants either some form of organizational and/or bargaining rights to various groups of public employees. These statutes differ substantially in the employee groups that they cover and often specify different rights for different groups of employees.[5] Table 2.1 below presents information concerning the various state statutes and some of the major provisions contained in those laws. The wide variation in extent and nature of the coverage of these statutes is striking. The most widely accepted collective bargaining is for public employees in public education, while only eighteen states have omnibus collective bargaining statutes that permit and/or protect collective bargaining rights for all public employees. Table 2.1 also presents information on which states protect rights for only state or professional employees and which states protect all public employee bargaining rights. The table further presents data concerning employees' rights to strike and the specification of impasse procedures in labor law.

Table 2.1 shows the states that protect, by statutory law, the collective bargaining rights of state and school district employees and those states that have omnibus (covering all state and local employees) laws. There are other states that permit collective

Table 2.1
Collective Bargaining Laws for Public Employees

State	State Employees	Omnibus	Professional Employees	Strike Protected	Binding Arbitration
Alabama	No	No	No	No	No
Alaska	Yes	No	Yes	No	No
Arizona	No	No	Meet & Confer	No	No
Arkansas	No	No	No	No	No
California	Yes	No	Yes	No	Yes
Colorado	No	No	No	No	No
Connecticut	Yes	No	Yes	No	Yes
Delaware	Yes	No	Yes	No	No
Florida	No	Yes	Yes	No	No
Georgia	No	No	No	No	No
Hawaii	Yes	Yes	Yes	Yes	Yes
Idaho	Yes	No	Yes	No	No
Illinois	Yes	No	Yes	Limited	Yes
Indiana	No	No	Yes	No	No
Iowa	No	Yes	No	No	Yes
Kansas	Yes	No	Yes	No	No
Kentucky	No	No	No	No	No
Louisiana	No	No	No	No	No
Maine	No	Yes	Yes	No	Limited
Maryland	Yes	No	Yes	No	No
Massachusetts	No	Yes	Yes	No	Yes
Michigan	No	Yes	Yes	Limited	Yes
Minnesota	No	Yes	Yes	Limited	Yes
Mississippi	No	No	No	No	No
Missouri	No	Yes	Meet & Confer	No	No
Montana	No	Yes	Yes	Yes	Yes
Nebraska	Yes	No	Yes	No	Yes

Table 2.1 cont.

State	State Employees	Omnibus	Professional Employees	Strike Protected	Binding Arbitration
Nevada	Yes	No	Yes	No	Yes
New Hampshire	No	Yes	Yes	No	No
New Jersey	No	Yes	Yes	No	Yes
New Mexico	No	Yes	Yes	No	No
New York	No	Yes	Yes	No	Yes
N. Carolina	No	No	No	No	No
N. Dakota	Yes	No	Yes	No	No
Ohio	No	Yes	Yes	Yes	Yes
Oklahoma	Yes	No	Yes	No	No
Oregon	No	Yes	Yes	Yes	Yes
Pennsylvania	No	Yes	Yes	Limited	Yes
Rhode Island	Yes	No	Yes	Limited	Yes
S. Carolina	No	No	No	No	No
S. Dakota	No	Yes	Yes	No	No
Tennessee	Yes	No	Yes	No	No
Texas	No	No	Meet & Confer	No	No
Utah	No	No	No	No	No
Vermont	Yes	No	Yes	No	No
Virginia	No	No	No	No	No
Washington	Yes	No	Yes	No	Yes
West Virginia	No	No	Yes	No	No
Wisconsin	No	Yes	Yes	No	Yes
Wyoming	No	No	No	No	No
TOTAL	15	18	35	9	22

bargaining for public employees but only through court cases or attorney general opinions (e.g., West Virginia in the case of state employees by attorney general's opinion).

There are several states that permit meet and confer rather than collective bargaining. This distinction is important. Under a collective bargaining law the parties must meet and confer with the purpose in mind of negotiating a contract that incorporates those issues, on which they can agree, over which they are authorized to bargain. A collective bargaining statute will also generally contain provisions requiring good faith bargaining and prohibiting unfair labor practices, and often impasse procedures. None of these items is typically included in a meet and confer law. Often, meet and confer laws will not even make provisions for an exclusive bargaining representative. Meet and confer statutes typically require an employer to inform employees or their representative of issues relevant to their employment status and require that the employer give the employees an opportunity to comment on the proposed actions. There is no requirement for either the employer or the union to bargain nor for the employer even to give consideration to the desires of the employees or their unions.

Meet and confer and collective bargaining are very different types of requirements. It is appropriate to view meet and confer as unilateral decision making by the employer with an opportunity for employees to express opinions, and to view collective bargaining as bilateral decision making—between the employer and the union. As can be readily seen from examination of Table 2.1, collective bargaining is what has been adopted in most jurisdictions, and only a relatively few states have opted for meet and confer and then only for select class of public employees, such as Texas.

There are nine states that protect public employee rights to strike in various forms and degrees. There are other states that permit strikes either through assessing minor penalties or in a de facto manner (e.g., New York).[6] There are twenty-two states that specify that final and binding arbitration is the last step in the impasse procedures, but there are other states that permit the parties to negotiate an impasse resolution procedure that may end in final and binding arbitration. Of the twenty-two states having final and binding arbitration, there are states that limit the applicability of this form of impasse resolution (e.g., Maine and Rhode Island for certain employees for wage issues). Table 2.1 clearly shows that there is a wide variation in the nature of the laws governing collective bargaining for state and local government employees.

ELECTION POLICIES

The organization and representation of employees is typically an important focal point of most collective bargaining laws. A few remarks concerning this aspect of labor law are in order before proceeding to the controls on the substance and conduct of negotiations.

Thirty-three states provide for employees' rights to exclusive bargaining representatives.[7] Exclusive bargaining representation is a single union or association that has the sole right and responsibility to represent all employees within the bargaining unit it was certified to represent. The right of representation is typically defined in the bargaining statute. It is relatively common that the bargaining law will grant the right of representation concerning the presentation and resolution of grievances and the negotiation of a contract including such issues for which the statute may provide. There is some variation on the issues of collective bargaining. Some statutes will provide laundry lists of issues, and others will define the issues of collective bargaining as the terms and conditions of employment (this issue is discussed further in the following sections of this chapter).

A bargaining unit is the group of employees the statute defines as having similar interests, skills, responsibilities (i.e., super-visory), the desires of the employees, management, and the labor organization and/or bargaining histories. Some state statutes may include other factors that must be considered, but those cited are consistent with the requirements found in Taft-Hartley. The Public Employment Relations Board (PERB) will establish appropriate bargaining units through the procedures consistent with the requirements of the state labor law.

One illustrative example of statutory language concerning public employees' rights and exclusive representation from a state statute may prove useful. The Minnesota Public Employment Relations Act, for example, states in pertinent part:

Section 179A.06 (2) Public employees have the right to form and join labor or employee organizations, and have the right not to form and join such organizations. Public employees in an appropriate bargaining unit have the right by secret ballot to designate an exclusive representative to negotiate grievances procedures and the terms and conditions of employment with their employer.[8]

For the most part, the policies and procedures developed by the states concerning the certification of exclusive bargaining representatives are similar in most respects to the policies and procedures developed by the National Labor Relations Board for application to the private sector under the Taft-Hartley Act. There are, of course, minor deviations due to specific statutory law in a few of the states. These deviations are not critical to the present discussion, and the reader is referred to Bureau of National Affairs, Labor Relations Reference Manual, State Labor Law, for further information and comparisons on the topic.

EMPLOYEE RIGHTS

Most state collective bargaining statutes specify certain rights public employees and their unions are granted by the law. This follows the lead set in the federal law for private sector employees under Section 7 of the Taft-Hartley Act. The rights enumerated in these state statutes are probably the most similar sections of all the provisions of the various state collective bargaining statutes. As is discussed in the following section, violation of these public employee rights by either the employer or union is an unfair labor practice and may be enjoined, and any employee unfairly fired will be ordered reinstated and may be awarded lost pay and benefits due to the wrongful discharge. These rights are why most collective bargaining statutes were enacted, to assure public employees these rights and to provide a mechanism by which these rights can be exercised.

Another illustrative example of statutory language from a specific state may prove useful. The Massachusetts public employee bargaining law contains a typical employees' rights section which states:

Sec. 2 [Right to organize and bargain]—Employees shall have the right of self-organization and the right to form, join, or assist any employee organization for the purpose of bargaining collectively through representatives of their own choosing on questions of wages, hours, and other terms and conditions of employment, and to engage in lawful, concerted activities for the purpose of collective bargaining or other mutual aid or protection, free from interference, restraint, or coercion. An employee shall have the right to refrain from any or all such activities, except to the extent of making such payment of service fees to an exclusive representative as provided in Sec. 12.[9]

The rights found in this section are individual rights of public employees. Most fundamental among these rights is that of the freedom to join, form, or assist a labor organization or to refrain from such activities. This right, often called concerted activity or self-help, is the key to effective labor unionization and collective bargaining. If guarantees of freedom from interference, restraint, or coercion for individual employees were not granted, then the remaining provisions would be meaningless.

UNFAIR LABOR PRACTICES

Most state statutes provide for the prohibition and remedy of certain collective bargaining practices deemed to be against the public policy of the state. These practices are generally action committed by either the labor organization or management that prevents collective bargaining from functioning or that denies the employees, management, or the union rights guaranteed by the statute.

Often a state will establish an administration law agency for the purpose of investigating and remedying unfair labor practices. These agencies, in general, have the authority and responsibility to administer the collective bargaining law and will normally conduct certification elections and administer the impasse procedures as well. Thirty-one states presently have such administrative law agencies.[10] The agencies, typically called the Public Employment Relations Board of Commission, have roughly the same responsibilities for the state laws as the National Labor Relations Board has for the Taft-Hartley Act.

Unfair labor practices are sometimes called prohibited practices and generally follow the proscriptions contained in the Taft-Hartley Act, but there are notable differences in some statutes. Kansas, for example, makes the interference in any employee organization by a public employer a prohibited practice, even in cases where there is no certified bargaining representative.[11] New York's Taylor Act contains the following unfair labor practice language:

Sec. 209-a. Improper employer practices; improper employee organization practices; application.—1. Improper employer practices. It shall be an improper practice for a public employer or its agents deliberately (a) to interfere with, restrain or coerce public employees in the exercise of their rights guaranteed in section two hundred two for the purpose of depriving them of such rights; (b) to dominate or interfere with the formation or administration of any employee organization for the purpose of depriving them of such rights; (c) to discriminate against any employee for the purpose of encouraging or discouraging membership in, or participation in the activities of, any employee organization; (d) to refuse to negotiate in good faith with the duly recognized or certified representatives of its public employees; or (e) to refuse to continue all the terms of an expired agreement until a new agreement is negotiated, unless the employee organization which is a party to such agreement has, during such negotiations or prior to such resolution of such negotiations, engaged in conduct violative of subdivision one of section two hundred ten of this article [prohibition of strikes].

2. Improper employee organization practices. It shall be an improper practice for an employee organization or its agents deliberately (a) to interfere with, restrain or coerce public employees in the exercise of the rights granted in section two hundred two, or to cause, or attempt to cause, a public employer to do so; or (b) to refuse to negotiate collectively in good faith with a public employer, provided it is the duly recognized or certified representative of the employees of such employer.

3. Application. In applying this section, fundamental distinctions between private and public employment shall be recognized, and no body of federal or state law applicable wholly or in part to private employment, shall be regarded as binding or controlling precedent.[12]

New York's Taylor Act is somewhat similar, in the unfair labor practices specified, to the Taft-Hartley Act. Paragraph 3 is of some note; this language specifically states that the precedents established under statutes governing private sector labor relations shall not be binding precedents under the Taylor Act. As with the Taft-Hartley Act, the New York Public Employment Relations Board has been specifically limited in the remedies it may impose to correct unfair labor practices.[13] Cease-and-desist orders and the reinstatement of wrongfully discharged employees (with or without back pay and benefits) is generally all that a PERB may impose as a remedy for an unfair labor practice.

The unfair labor practice provisions are what gives teeth to a collective bargaining law. Those activities most detrimental to the formation of labor organizations and the proper operation of negotiations are prohibited by the unfair labor practice provisions of the various state laws. The enforcement of these provisions is only made possible by the creation of an administrative law agency. Without the unfair labor practice provisions contained in a collective bargaining law, that law would be meaningless. The unfair labor practice provisions and their enforcement procedures are what make the collective bargaining statute work.

SCOPE OF BARGAINING

The scope of bargaining is defined as the range of issues that must be or may be negotiated by the parties. Under the Taft-Hartley Act the scope of bargaining is divided into two groups of issues for bargaining and one set of issues over which bargaining is illegal.[14] The two groups of issues over which bargaining occurs are divided into mandatorily negotiable items and issues over which bargaining is voluntary. A mandatory issue of collective bargaining is a term and condition of employment under the Taft-Hartley Act, and a voluntary issue of bargaining is either an item said to be at the core of entrepreneurial discretion, or in the case of a labor organization, an internal union affair. The latter category of issues may not be bargained to an impasse under the federal statute. There are those states that follow the same scheme of determining the scope of bargaining; for example, the following section from the California Public Employment Relations Act in pertinent part states:

Sec. 3504. The scope of representation shall include all matters relating to employment conditions and employer–employee relations, including but not limited to, wages, hours, and other terms and conditions of employment, except, however, that the scope of bargaining shall not include consideration of the merits, necessity, or organization of any service or activity provided by law or executive order.[15]

This California statute shows that essentially the same language as is found in Section 8 (d) of the Taft-Hartley Act was adopted by the State of California, except that those items required to be fixed under the authority of other statutes or executive orders are not subject to collective bargaining. Since various state constitutions or statutes require certain decisions to be retained by the legislative or executive branches of government, this California language is illustrative of the problems encountered in determining the scope of collective bargaining in the public sector. There are, however, other states that have specified laundry lists of issues subject to collective bargaining (e.g., Kansas). There are also states that do not differentiate between mandatory or voluntary issues of collective bargaining.

OTHER LEGAL PROVISIONS

There are numerous other provisions often contained in state collective bargaining statutes. Impasse resolution procedures, for example, are often specified in state collective bargaining laws. These impasse resolution procedures are statutory mechanisms for resolving disputes over the negotiation of a contract. These provisions are discussed in detail beginning later in this book and will not be given further attention here.

Most state collective bargaining laws offer sections defining terms for purposes of the statute. These definitional sections often contain some important substantive provisions. The manner in which a bargaining unit is to be determined and who is eligible for inclusion in such bargaining units are generally found in these definitions. The bargaining unit, as was discussed above, is the group of employees who may vote in a certification election, and if the union is certified as exclusive bargaining representation it is these eligible voters whom the union must then represent. The nature of this representation and the standards used to make these determinations are also typically included in these definitional sections of state bargaining statutes.

State collective bargaining statutes often differentiate between various classes of employees (e.g., Ohio differentiates between public safety and other employees; California differentiates between employees of the University of California and California State University in its Higher Education Bargaining Law). These differentiations often allow certain employees the use of different impasse procedures, may limit or authorize strikes, or even specify that certain issues of bargaining are not protected for certain employees. These differentiations are due to the various occupations covered by a collective bargaining law. It is not uncommon for police, firefighters, sanitation workers, and public school teachers to be covered by the same law (e.g., Ohio). Such differences in occupations typically result in differences in bargaining rights as can easily be seen from an examination of Table 2.1.

Union security arrangements are often limited by state collective bargaining laws. For example, Nevada provides for collective bargaining rights for public employees but prohibits union security arrangements. Union security arrangements, commonly referred to as union or agency shop, are contract provisions that require employees to join the union after a specified period of employment (union shop), or in lieu of joining the union, tender a service fee equal to the dues and fees charged union members (agency shop). In some cases, the state public employment collective bargaining law will reference another statute, commonly called a right-to-work law, that prohibits such union security arrangements for all bargaining relations in the state regardless of whether in the private or public sector.

Approximately twenty-two states prohibit or limit union security arrangements for public employee unions.[16] These states are almost all either southern states or those with an agrarian economy. Virtually none of the northern industrial states has such prohibitions of union security arrangements.

THE EFFECT OF THE LEGAL ENVIRONMENT ON COLLECTIVE BARGAINING

As should now be obvious to even the most casual observer, there are substantial constraints placed on the parties as well as several rights guaranteed to the respective parties by the various state labor laws. In the extreme, those states that prohibit public employee collective bargaining impose upon public employees a system of labor–management relations that is inconsistent with the treatment of the majority of public employees in the United States. A significant number of employees in the private sector are also unionized, and the majority are covered by Taft-Hartley. Those employees without the protection of a collective bargaining statute are subjected to the unilateral determination of the terms and conditions of employment by management or the legislative branch of government. Thirty-five other states have chosen various forms of bilateral determination of various issues, including the terms and conditions of employment, at least in part. This leaves approximately twelve states that have not taken legislative action on the subject of public sector collective bargaining. A few of these states permit collective bargaining either in a de facto manner or because of an attorney general's opinion or court case. In the case of Indiana, the governor issued an executive order protecting collective bargaining for state employees. In these twelve states there are no unfair labor practices, administrative law agencies, or definitions of the scope of bargaining that can serve as a guide to assure peaceful and reasonable collective bargaining. In the thirty-five states with bargaining statutes, most provide the bare necessities for an orderly collective bargaining system. Only four of these thirty-five states do not have a Public Employment Relations Board charged with responsibilities of administering the state law.[17]

The most obvious effects of these statutes is whether or not striking is permitted. If striking is permitted, both parties are free to test their relative bargaining power by the union striking and/or the employer locking out. In those statutes where strikes and lockouts are prohibited, a substitute for the proscribed economic warfare is generally provided through either statutory or voluntary impasse resolution procedures. These impasse procedures have the potential of influencing the behavior of negotiators and have the general effect of insulating the public from the inconveniences associated with a work stoppage.

The issues that must be and may be negotiated are typically defined in detail in the statute. The issues included within the scope of bargaining will help to shape the final product as well as the course of negotiations. In jurisdictions with limited bargaining scopes there will be fewer substantive issues that may be negotiated.

The rights guaranteed public employees by these statutes may influence the scope of bargaining as well as its conduct. If the law provides for certain rights, such as due process if discharged, then the need to negotiate those rights into the contract is mitigated; this limits the scope of bargaining. If a statute fails to provide assurances from failures to bargain in good faith, then there is an obvious and predictable effect on the conduct of negotiations. The rights guaranteed public employees under the state statutes are almost uniform and are, for the most part, consistent with those rights guaranteed private sector employees. The real differences occur with respect to the issues subject to collective bargaining and the right to strike as well as the impasse procedures for those employees who are denied the right to strike. The nature of the collective bargaining will vary, state by state, with the requirements of law.[18] It is therefore important that the reader bear in mind that there are substantial differences in the legal environments of the various states.

SUMMARY AND CONCLUSIONS

The public sector, federal, state, and local governments, are not governed by the Taft-Hartley Act. For state and local employers and employees, coverage of some labor law depends on state or local legislative action. Thirty-five states have enacted some form of labor law protecting public employers and public employees. Three states have prohibited public employee collective bargaining.

There is a wide variation in the nature of public sector collective bargaining laws. Some jurisdictions have enacted omnibus statutes that protect the bargaining rights of all employees. Professional teaching employees have the widest coverage of collective bargaining statutes. The majority of states prohibit strikes by public employees, and almost half of the states provide for the final and binding arbitration of contract disputes. Some states, such as Ohio and Illinois, allow strikes under certain circumstances but also provide for procedures to resolve contract disputes.

The majority of state collective bargaining laws guarantee public employees the right to form, join, and assist labor organizations for the purpose of collective bargaining. Most of these statutes provide for rights that are very similar to those granted private sector employees under the Taft-Hartley Act and are fairly consistent from jurisdiction to jurisdiction. The violation of these public employee rights are generally proscribed as unfair labor practices.

Most state statutes provide for an administrative law agency whose function it is to determine appropriate bargaining units, conduct certification elections, and administer the unfair labor practice provisions of the law. Most state statutes provide for certain employer and union activities to be against the public policy and allow the administrative law agency (e.g., PERB) to remedy the prohibited practice through injunctions or reinstatement ordered for wrongfully discharged employees. The unfair labor practice provisions and election policies and procedures under most state statutes are relatively uniform across jurisdictions and are generally similar to those found in the Taft-Hartley Act, but there are notable exceptions (i.e., New York and Kansas), but even these exceptions do not deviate far from the Taft-Hartley example.

The scope of collective bargaining refers to those issues subject to collective bargaining. Many state statutes provide that the terms and conditions of employment are mandatory issues of bargaining. Some state statutes provide laundry lists of items that are mandatorily negotiable, and some even provide for definitions of voluntary issues of bargaining. The various states are not consistent in their handling of the scope of bargaining, and wide variations can be found.

As should be obvious with the amount of variation present in the state statutes, the legal environment may differ significantly from state to state. It is likely that the conduct of negotiations and their results will be effected by these differing legal environments. This should be expected to result in different bargaining relations between states and provide for a lack of consistency in the collective bargaining observed across state and local government.

NOTES

1. Labor Management Relations Act of 1947, cited as National Labor Relations Act as amended, (commonly called Taft-Hartley Act after its authors) 61 Stat. 136.

2. For further discussion see Charles O. Gregory and Harold A. Katz, *Labor and the Law*, 3d ed. (New York: Norton Publishing Company, 1979), 599–606.

3. Benjamin J. Taylor and Fred Witney, *Labor Relations Law*, 4th ed. (Englewood Cliffs, N.J.: Prentice-Hall, Inc., 1983), 647.

4. These states are Texas, North Carolina, and Virginia.

5. Indiana, for example, has a statute protecting collective bargaining rights for teachers but it prohibited collective bargaining for state employees until an executive order issued by the governor in 1990.

6. This topic will be discussed in greater detail in Chapter 9.

7. Bureau of National Affairs, Labor Relations Reference Manual, State Labor Laws.

8. Chapter 179A of Minnesota Statutes, as amended, effective May 21, 1985.

9. Chapter 150E, Section 2, Massachusetts Laws 1986.

10. Bureau of National Affairs, Labor Relations Reference Manual, State Labor Laws.

11. Kansas Statutes Annotated 75–4333 (b) (1), Kansas Public Employer–Employee Relations Act.

12. Sections 200 to 214 of the Civil Service Law of New York, commonly known as the Taylor Act, last amended June 30, 1985.

13. *Board of Supervisors v. PERB*, NY CtApp (1975), 89 LRRM 2713.

14. *NLRB v. Wooster Division of Borg-Warner Corporation*, 356 U.S. 342 (1958).

15. Sections 3500 through 3510 of the California Government Code, last amended October 16, 1981.

16. Bureau of National Affairs, Labor Relations Reference Manual, State Labor Laws.

17. Ibid.

18. See Thomas A. Kochan, *Collective Bargaining and Industrial Relations* (Homewood, Ill.: Richard D. Irwin, Inc., 1980), Chapter 4 for further discussion.

3

The Public Sector and Collective Bargaining

The 1960s was a critical period for collective bargaining in the public sector. In 1962 the first state collective bargaining statute was enacted in Wisconsin, and President Kennedy issued a landmark executive order protecting bargaining rights for federal employees. Since the middle of that decade the public sector has been the fastest growing employment sector in the U.S. economy.

The role of government is controversial in the United States. The recent conservative political successes are testimony to the views of government held by the citizens of this country. Collective bargaining has also become increasingly controversial over the past decade. Collective bargaining in the public sector is therefore a wedding of two controversial institutions.

The purpose of this chapter is to lay a foundation upon which to build an understanding of labor law. It first examines the growth of the importance of government in the U.S. economic system, and then turns attention to an examination of collective bargaining in the public sector from a philosophical perspective.

THE PUBLIC SECTOR

Despite changes in the magnitude of the public sector as well as in the relative importance of different revenue sources, one thing that has not changed since the time of Adam Smith is the basic nature of government services. All of them can be classified into two categories. First, there are those services that would not be provided at all if not by the state. Here, either capital requirements for the service far exceed the financial resources of private individuals to provide the service or, if within the financial abilities of private providers, the inability to exclude nonpaying individuals from benefits (i.e., the existence of what economists call external economies) renders provision of the service unprofitable. The impact of external economies upon private provision can be illustrated by means of a simple private sector example. Two homeowners with a common property line desire to enclose their backyards with chain-link fence. Aware that the homeowner who postpones fencing the yard until the other homeowner's fence is in place can realize substantial savings by "tying" into the fence along the common property line, both homeowners delay installation of the fence, which is thus constructed only after great delay or not constructed at all. In either case, the existence of external economies (i.e., the inability to exclude nonpaying individuals from the benefits of a good or service financed by another) has hampered private production of the good. The classic example of a service that falls into this category of government services is national defense. Resource requirements and external economies both preclude its provision by the private sector.

The second category of government services includes all services that would not be provided in sufficient volume if left exclusively to the private sector. Quite simply, the market system would price such services beyond the reach of many residents. To guarantee provision of the socially optimum volume of these essential services, society subsidizes their production through taxation. Examples most often cited are education, police protection, and fire protection. Also included in this category are services intended to remedy the failure of the private sector to account fully for all costs of private production. Here, the price of the product does not reflect total production cost; part of the cost of production has been shifted to society as a whole by way of air, water, and land pollution. Societal concern for diseconomies, as these costs are commonly called, has led to a complex system of government standards, rules, and regulations designed to internalize the costs, thereby protecting the environment for all citizens.

The Classic View of the Public Sector

The influence wielded by all levels of government in today's economy presents a stark contrast to the very limited role for government envisioned by Adam Smith 200 years ago. Writing in 1776, the "Father of Modern Economics" stated that the state has but three legitimate functions, namely:

that of protecting the society from the violence and invasion of other independent societies . . . [1]

that of protecting as far as possible, every member of the society from the injustice of oppression of every other member of it, or the duty of establishing an exact administration of justice . . . [2]

that of erecting and maintaining those public institutions and those public works, which, though they may be in the highest degree advantageous to a great society, are, however, of such a nature, that the profit could never repay the expense of any individual or small number of individuals, and which it therefore cannot be expected that any individual or small number of individuals should erect or maintain.[3]

The first two duties are self-explanatory. By the third, Adam Smith meant provision of institutions "facilitating the commerce of society and those promoting the instruction of people"—roads, bridges, canals, harbors, and schools.[4] Only the most limited role for government was envisioned. As society became more complex and interrelated, the role of government has become greater and more extensive.

Funding of government services was of particular concern to Smith. While national defense "should be defrayed by the general contribution of the whole society," general tax revenue should not be the primary source of support for other government services.[5] With regard to the administration of justice:

The whole expense of justice too might easily be defrayed by the fees of court; and, without exposing the administration of justice to any real hazard of corruption, the public revenue might thus be entirely discharged from a certain, though perhaps, but small incumbrance.[6]

Payment for public works, in Smith's view, would be accomplished by taxing those who benefit from the works and user fees:

It does not seem necessary that the expense of those public works should be defrayed from that public revenue, as it is commonly called . . . The greater part of such public works may be easily managed, as to afford a particular revenue sufficient for defraying their own expense, without bringing any burden upon the general revenue of society.[7]

The financing of education was also viewed by Smith as being a user fee paid for a private service:

The institutions for education of the youth may, in the same manner, furnish a revenue sufficient for defraying their own expense. The fee or honorary which a scholar pays to the master naturally constitutes a revenue of this kind.[8]

Smith's preoccupations with user fees and taxes to finance non-defense-related state expenditures stemmed from his concern for equity and efficiency. According to Smith, the use of general revenue to support specific government services increased the likelihood of corruption, inefficiency, and waste. Without a user fee, consumers (i.e., citizens) lack an effective leverage mechanism to guarantee the types and quality of services desired; services are dependent upon general tax revenue and not upon consumer approval, and there was only an imperfect substitute for the market to determine the proper allocation of resources—that being the political system.

Unique Characteristics of the Public Employer

Critical to any analysis of public sector collective bargaining and the problems attendant thereto is an understanding of the similarities and differences between public and private employers. All employers execute contracts with their employees whereby the employees agree to accept direction and to render specified labor services toward achievement of employer-set goals in exchange for wages and salaries. Beyond this basic exchange function, however, private and public employers share very little in common. The environment within which goals are determined and employees are directed differs significantly for public and private employers. Differences in the source of decision-making authority and in the service-delivery mechanism are primarily responsible for the environmental dichotomy between private and public employers. Decision making in the public sector is far more diffused than it is in the private sector. The delivery system for public goods and services is far more indirect and less market driven than for private goods and services. Each of these differences is reviewed in the following paragraphs.

Sovereignty

Property rights constitute the source of decision-making authority in the private sector. The right to direct a business enterprise is based upon ownership of property and the constitutional guarantees to own and use that property. Management serves at the pleasure of the property owners and acts in the interests of the owners of the capital.

On the other hand, it is the people who constitute the source of decision-making authority in the public sector. Sovereignty, "the supreme, absolute, and uncontrolled power by which any independent state is governed," rests with the people.[9] Decision-making authority flows in an upward direction from the people to various levels of government that, in turn, exercise this sovereign power on behalf of the people. The traditional "position on sovereignty maintains that government has sole authority which cannot be given to, taken by, or shared with anyone" because government is the designated caretaker of that sovereignty.[10] Government is the designated caretaker of that sovereignty because the people have entrusted their ultimate decision-making authority in the government.

The sovereignty doctrine no longer enjoys the popularity it once did as an argument against collective bargaining in the public sector. In the first place, given the execution of government contracts with various business groups wherein terms and conditions are bilaterally determined, the argument is at best convoluted and at worst, given the government's active encouragement of employees in the private sector to challenge managerial authority, smacks of duplicity. Second, the force of the argument has been reduced to the extent that various governmental units have voluntarily recognized and bargained with public employee unions. Finally, the sovereign power of government has been limited by legislation and court decision in non-labor-relations matters (e.g., the 1948 Tucker Act permitting contract suits against the federal government).[11] Logic would seem to warrant a similar limitation of sovereignty in the labor relations arena when justified by the public interest—as indeed has occurred at the federal and state levels where executive orders and statutes permit organizations and bargaining. Despite its decreased overall popularity, the sovereignty concept nonetheless remains a convenient, albeit not very convincing, philosophical argument advanced by government officials and others who fear "that collective bargaining would infringe on management prerogatives, weaken authority, and affect adversely the efficiency of government operations."[12]

Diffused Nature of Public Decision-Making Authority

The checks-and-balances system designed to provide a balancing and oversight of the power of any political division is also a source of inefficiency and frustration in decision making in the public sector. In private enterprise, the structure of the organization is one that promotes efficiency and control. The private business enterprise is also profit-motivated, thereby giving a clear measure of success and viability. A corporate chief executive officer is the decision-making authority and can readily delegate that authority as he or she sees fit. Government has no profit motive, hence no direct test of success. Government is structured not for efficiency but also to assure that abuse of power will be observed and offset by another branch of government. Further, the decision makers are either elected or answer to elected officials; this fact bring a political dimension to public sector decisions that do not exist in the private sector.

Separation of power and its harmful effects upon bargaining have been advanced as arguments against collective bargaining by public employees. To argue that a process should not be implemented simply because implementation is difficult is equivalent to throwing the baby out with the bath water; it is simply not convincing. Granted, diffusion of authority imposes certain costs, but these as well as other costs should be evaluated in context of the benefits associated with joint employee-employer decision making before any decision is made. One benefit often overlooked in regard to the relationship between collective bargaining and separation of power is the increased accountability (efficiency) on the part of public sector managers that results from bargaining-induced clarification of the lines of management authority. Also not to be forgotten is the fact that unions encountered a similarly frustrating problem when bargaining in the private sector commenced on a wide scale in the 1930s. The question "Who is management within the framework of a complicated corporate structure?" has since been satisfactorily resolved.

Public Service Delivery System

In many respects, the private employer is like a juggler who must call upon a variety of skills and talents to perform successfully. Long-term survival requires the private employer to ascertain consumer tastes and preferences, to organize and combine factor inputs to produce the types of goods and services consumers desire, and to set a price that consumers will pay and that will cover costs of production. As in the case of the juggler, failure in any area will spell disaster for the private employer. The precarious position the private employer occupies in market economy is the trade-off between competitiveness in the market-place and the ability to pay workers a living wage and induce greater productivity.

By contrast, the public employer operates within a relatively risk-free, secure environment. The needs of consumers are iden-tified through established political process and serviced through government's ability to tax. Operating in such an environment, the public employer is not subject to the same constraints that the private employer is subject to during bargaining. Neither the need to earn a normal profit nor to maintain a market position inhibits the public employer's strategies during bargaining. For, by nature and definition, the public employer is nonprofit and the sole provider of the service.

FACTORS RESPONSIBLE FOR GROWTH OF THE PUBLIC SECTOR

Having touched upon the present-day public sector, the lim-ited role for government envisioned by Adam Smith, and the basic nature of government services, we turn now to the factors responsible for the phenomenal growth in the public sector. Three factors share responsibility for this growth. First, the external diseconomies associated with economic growth have expanded government's role by exacerbating longstanding public problems (e.g., drugs, congestion, public health) and by creating new problems (e.g., pollution). Thus, economic growth has increased the intensity as well as the number of problems within the public domain.

Second, as real income levels have risen during the course of economic growth, services have become a proportionately more important component of aggregate demand. In the jargon of economists, the demand for services is said to have become "income elastic." As an integral part of the service sector of the economy, government has shared in this income-driven growth. In addition, rising levels of affluence have prompted individuals to delegate greater responsibility for services traditionally provided, for the most part, by the private sector (e.g., health care, welfare, etc.) to various levels of government. In a real sense, it could be said that social consciousness and generosity are also income elastic.

Finally, and most importantly, society's propensity to accord the state a broader role in the economy has not been checked, until recently, by that factor that limits demand in the private sector, namely, price. Reliance upon general revenues instead of user fees to finance government services, the consequent diffusion of cost over a large tax-paying public, the temporal separation between provision of a public service and payment for that service by way of general taxes, and the seemingly limitless ability of government to defray cost through borrowing, have all combined to create the erroneous impression that government services are a bargain, if not "free,"—thus stimulating overconsumption and overproduction. In short, widely used methods of funding have masked the real costs of government services and have thereby pushed society in the direction of an expanded role for government. In light of the foregoing discussion, Adam Smith's earlier noted preoccupation with user taxes and fees becomes eminently more understandable.

IMPLICATIONS FOR LABOR LAW

The changing attitudes toward government, its sovereignty, and role in society have resulted not only in its growth but also on greater reliance on public services. The growth of the public sector and its increased importance, especially in areas where it has a monopoly, makes peaceful labor relations more critical than in past decades. This same growth in government also makes agencies much larger, and the management problems attendant thereto are the primary causes of unionization. Further, the increased employment in the public sector also creates a philosophical difficulty in not providing a significant proportion of the U.S. workforce with the same bargaining rights enjoyed by federal and private sector employees.

State legislatures have followed the lead of the federal government and enacted statutes that assure collective bargaining rights for public employees. This has resulted from the changing philosophical foundations of government. With the demise of the sovereignty doctrine has come the understanding that public employees have the same goals and needs as private sector employees. As people have become more used to the idea that government is not a simple extension of the voting public, resistance to unionization of public employees has declined. State legislatures have enacted collective bargaining statutes at an increasing rate in response to these significant philosophical and political changes.

There is also a basic matter of equity. The voting public and hence legislatures have developed an understanding that collective bargaining is the manner by which industrial democracy occurs in the U.S. economic system. State legislatures have been willing, in numerous cases, to permit public employees in their jurisdictions to become full participants in the U.S. economy.

SUMMARY AND CONCLUSIONS

The classic philosophical view of government was that it was to have a very limited role. Where possible, governmental services should be financed by user fees, and taxes should be imposed only on the segments of society that truly benefit from the public good or service. The presently held view of government is far less restrictive.

Public goods and services are required because of diseconomies of private production, they are income elastic, and society has come to accept the government's borrowing as an almost unlimited source of goods and services. These phenonemona have resulted in significant growth in the public sector. With the growth has come the attendant problems of large size, impersonal relations, and inefficiency that breeds unionization. State legislatures have reacted to these factors and have passed enabling legislation so that public sector employees at the state and local levels can join their counterparts in the federal and private sector and be represented by unions for purposes of collective bargaining.

NOTES

1. Adam Smith, *The Wealth of Nations*, Cannan Edition (New York: The Modern Library, Inc., 1937), 653.
2. Ibid., 669.
3. Ibid., 681.
4. Ibid.
5. Ibid., 787.
6. Ibid., 677–678.
7. Ibid., 682.
8. Ibid., 716.
9. Michael H. Moscow, J. J. Loewenberg, and Edward J. Kazaria, *Collective Bargaining in Public Employment* (New York: Random House, 1970), 16–17.
10. Ibid., 17.
11. Ibid.
12. Ibid., 18.

II

The Law

4

Administrative Law Agencies and Their Functions

There are states that permit collective bargaining for public employees but provide no enabling legislation. In the absence of legislation there are no procedures for the certification of bargaining representatives and the enforcement of the parties' respective rights. States that have enacted collective bargaining laws have established administrative law agencies for the purpose of enforcing the law and providing orderly procedures to certify bargaining representatives, to resolve impasses, and to enforce the parties' respective rights.

The structure and functions of administrative law agencies is the focus of this chapter. The first section of this chapter introduces the reader to administrative law agencies, the second section is concerned with the structure of these agencies, and the third section is a discussion of the functions of these agencies.

ADMINISTRATIVE LAW AGENCIES

Every state that has a collective bargaining law also has an administrative law agency responsible for the oversight and enforcement of the law. These agencies have various titles (e.g., Indiana Educational Employment Relations Board, Kansas Public Employee Relations Board, New Jersey Public Employment Relations Commission, or Michigan Employment Relations Commission) but basically have the same types of structures and roles.

The creation of statutory rights requires that there be a mechanism for the enforcement of those rights. Hard and bitter lessons were learned during the early days of the New Deal that demonstrated the necessity of enforcement procedures and mechanisms. The courts are slow, expensive, and limited only to the resolution of controversies arising concerning the interpretation and application of these laws. Yet, more is required if the collective bargaining envisioned by state legislatures is to be effective. Reliance on voluntary compliance was demonstrated under the National Labor Board (NLB), created by the National Industrial Recovery Act, to be ineffective. The National Labor Board had no statutory procedures upon which to rely and consequently was forced to create its own procedures and attempt to gain party acceptability for its creations. The inability of the National Labor Board to seek enforcement simply completed the cycle of ineffectiveness. As Taylor and Witney observed:

By February 1934, mainly as a result of its futile efforts to settle the *Weirton* and *Budd* disputes on the basis of the Reading Formula, the National Labor Board was on the verge of collapse. The example had been set by *Weirton* and *Budd* for others to follow. Orders of the Board were not respected and its authority was disregarded. Because the peaceful procedures of the Board had broken down, the frequency of organizational strikes increased sharply. Workers and employers were both determined to prevail in organizational contests. Since the National Labor Board could not control the situation by holding elections, employees resorted to the strike to gain their objective.

Enforcement of the law is a necessary prerequisite to its effectiveness. The administrative law agency must exist to operate the mechanisms necessary to conduct certification elections, to investigate and resolve unfair labor practice complaints, and to administer impasse procedures. In addition, the administrative law agency must also have the ability to make its decisions binding upon the parties. This is accomplished only through court orders in a civilized society. The lessons of the 1930s are reflected in the Wagner Act. Congress established statutory procedures, thereby relieving the National Labor Relations Board (NLRB) from the responsibility to attempt to fashion effective machinery. Congress also contemplated the parties' lack of voluntary compliance and authorized the NLRB to seek enforcement of its decisions by the courts. Again, the lessons learned by the National Labor Relations Board are readily apparent in the various state statutes in evidence today.

STRUCTURE OF ADMINISTRATIVE LAW AGENCIES

The structure of the various administrative law agencies does not differ substantially from the structure observed for the NLRB as it was originally constituted under the Wagner Act. The breath of the jurisdiction of the NLRB does create a difference in the administrative elements between itself and the various state agencies. For example, the Office of the General Counsel exists under the NLRB to prosecute unfair labor practice claims that have been investigated and found worthy of litigation. Most state boards have no counterpart to the Office of the General Counsel. Under most state bargaining laws the petitioner and respondent provide their own legal counsel. The state boards provide counsel only when enforcement of a board becomes necessary.

NLRB members are appointed by the president for five-year terms. State statutes vary, but in general the governor of the state appoints members to the administrative law agency, and they too serve set terms. The composition of the state agencies generally follows the lead of the NLRB, and the majority of such boards have five members.

Decision Making and Administration

The administrative law agency is typically divided into two entities. There is the board or commission that is the policy-making body and appellant authority. This board or commission is the governing body for the board or commission and comprises the appointed members. The remaining entity is the administrative staff, which typically includes a director, field examiners/investigators, adjudicators, and clerical staff. Its function is to conduct certification/decertification elections, investigate and adjudicate prohibited-practice complaints, and it often has specific responsibilities in statutory impasse procedures. In several states the decision-making authority for prohibited-practice complaints and bargaining unit determinations are reserved specifically to the board and may not be delegated, while other states permit delegation to administrative officers.

The administrative law agencies also generally provide for educational activities through conferences, seminars, and training programs for labor relations practitioners. These activities exist when the statute grants the agency the authority to take what actions will effectuate the purposes of the act. Education is often presumed to be effective in preventing disputes, and agencies will pursue educational activities for this purpose.

The administrative portion of an administrative law agency provides direct service to the parties to collective bargaining, but are also the support element for the board itself. The director is responsible to assign investigators to cases and decisions to adjudicate unfair labor practice cases. In some jurisdictions, the decision to adjudicate remains with the board. The establishment of bargaining units and the conduct of election procedures also falls to the director.

Administrative Agency for
Impasse Procedures

Impasse procedures vary significantly from state to state. In some jurisdictions the administrative law agency has virtually no role to play in impasse resolution. In other jurisdictions, the administrative law agency may provide mediators and serve as the administrative agency for fact finding and arbitration. New Jersey, Iowa, and New York maintain lists of competent neutrals to serve as mediators, fact finders, and/or arbitrators from which the parties may select a neutral to assist in resolving bargaining impasses.

Placement of Agency in Governmental Structure

In several cases the administrative law agency is an independent entity and is funded separately from other state agencies, for example in Iowa. In Kansas, the Kansas Public Employee Relations Board (KPERB) is not an independent entity. The director of KPERB reports not only to the PERB but is also a part of the Department of Human Resources, and the director also reports to the secretary of the Department of Human Resources.

When the administrative law agency is a part of the Department of Human Resources or similar cabinet-level entity, the board may be responsible for more than public sector labor relations. Again, the KPERB has responsibilities for the state's wage and hour act and is also responsible for the inspection of boilers in public buildings. When a PERB is an independent entity there are no responsibilities added on as in the case of Iowa.

Kansas has had particular problems with this structure. After service under both Republican and Democrat administrations, the position of director of the Kansas PERB was administratively changed to permit a newly elected governor to change significantly the director functions and duties. By so doing, the governor of Kansas significantly reduced the position's compensation and appointed a political supporter to this position. The effectiveness of the Kansas PERB suffered, and the one-term governor was defeated. The newly elected governor is in the process of correcting the problems. Without independence, an administrative law agency can become a political football to the detriment of both organized labor and public agencies.

Composition of the Board

The final significant variation in administrative law agencies is the composition of the board. Most boards comprise individuals who are appointed because they hold a position of neutrality and are knowledgeable concerning either the law or labor relations. There are, however, tripartite boards. In Kansas, for example, the PERB consists of two members appointed by the governor from nominees offered by organized labor, two from the ranks of management, and a neutral who is acceptable to both management and labor representatives. Tripartite boards are relatively rare, with most states opting for a panel of neutrals.

FUNCTIONS OF THE ADMINISTRATIVE LAW AGENCIES

In general the functions of an administrative law agency will be those elements necessary for carrying out the legislative intent in passing the collective bargaining statute. The reason for the agency is to assure that the rights and obligations imposed on the parties are effective and that peaceful labor relations will be facilitated by the law; there is simply no other reason for administrative law agencies to be created. The legislative identification of functions places clear limits on the authority of the agency and also details what minimum obligations are expected of it.

Legislative Enumeration of Authority

The state collective bargaining statute will specifically identify the functions the legislature envisioned for the administrative law agency. The functions of the Board for Higher Education

Employer–Employee Relations Act in California are as follows:

This chapter shall be administered by the Public Employment Relations Board. In administering this chapter the board shall have all of the following rights, powers, duties and responsibilities.

(a) To determine in disputed cases, or otherwise approve appropriate units.

(b) To determine in disputed cases whether a particular item is within or without the scope of representation.

(c) To arrange for and supervise representation elections which shall be conducted by means of secret ballot elections, and to certify the results of the elections.

(d) To establish lists of persons representative of the public and qualified by experience to be available to serve as mediators, arbitrators, and factfinders. In no case shall such lists include persons who are on the staff of the board.

(e) To establish by regulation appropriate procedures for review of proposals to change unit determinations.

(f) To adopt, pursuant to Chapter 4.5 (commencing with Section 11371) of Part I of Division 3 of Title 2, rules and regulations to carry out the provisions and effectuate the purposes and policies of this chapter.

(g) To hold hearings, subpoena witnesses, administer oaths, take the testimony or deposition of any person, and, in connection therewith, to issue subpoenas duces tecum to require the production and examination of any employer's or employee organization's records, books, or papers relating to any matter within its jurisdiction, except for those records, books, or papers confidential under statute.

(h) To investigate unfair practice charges or alleged violations of this chapter, and to take such action and make such determinations in respect of such charges or alleged violations as the board deems necessary to effectuate the policies of this chapter.

(i) To bring an action in a court of competent jurisdiction to enforce any of its orders, decisions or rulings or to enforce the refusal to obey a subpoena. Upon issuance of a complaint charging that any person has engaged in or is engaging in an unfair practice, the board may petition the court for appropriate temporary relief or restraining order.

(j) To delegate its power to any member of the board or to any person appointed by the board for the performance of its functions, except that no fewer than two board members may participate in the determination of any ruling or decision on the merits of any dispute coming before it and except that a decision to refuse to issue a complaint shall require the approval of two board members.

(k) To decide contested matters involving recognition, certification, or decertification of employee organizations.

(l) To consider and decide issues relating to rights, privileges, and duties of an employee organization in the event of a merger, amalgamation, or transfer of jurisdiction between two or more employee organizations.

(m) To take such other action as the board deems necessary to discharge its powers and duties and otherwise to effectuate the purposes of this chapter.[2]

The functions of the California Public Employment Relations Board with respect to institutions of higher education are specifically delineated in paragraphs (a) through (l). Paragraph (m) also charges the board with other such actions as will effectuate the purposes of the act. While not uncommon, this language grants the board very broad authority in dealing with standard labor relations matters.

The California example also serves to demonstrate that administrative law agencies are required to investigate and to conduct hearings. Investigations concerning the determination of appropriate bargaining units for certification procedures are common to all collective bargaining statutes. The decision-making authority on unit determinations and unfair practices are reserved to the board, but the adjudicators and investigators will play major roles in the gathering of evidence so that the board can determine whether complaints should be issued or units defined in specific ways.

It is also clear that the board has the authority to issue subpoenas and to seek enforcement in the courts of its decisions (Paragraph [i]). These powers are also universal among state administrative law agencies.

Jurisdiction

The functions of the administrative law agency are brought to bear only within a context. The jurisdiction of an administrative law agency is therefore of some importance. The California example is again instructive. In that state the Higher Education Act is administered by the Public Employment Relations Board. The Educational Employees and Public Employees Act are also administered by the same board in California. Therefore the jurisdiction of the California PERB cuts across several statutes covering several types of public agencies. In Kansas, both statutes (education and public employees) are also administered by the same board. In Illinois, the public employee and the education bargaining statutes are administered by different administrative law agencies; there is substantial variation across states concerning what is expected of the board.

Private and Public?

The California example shows that a single agency can be made responsible for several bargaining statutes. This raises an interesting question concerning the jurisdiction of administrative law agencies. The National Labor Relations Act applies to firms in interstate commerce; however, those firms that do not appreciably effect commerce are not granted jurisdiction by the NLRB. The NLRB applies dollar standards to determine whether jurisdiction will be asserted, so many small businesses do not have Taft-Hartley coverage. This has created a potential for states to regulate both public and private labor relations under the same agency.

A quick review of private sector law concerning jurisdiction is instructive. The federal courts have limited what states can do in regulating labor relations. In 1957 the U.S. Supreme Court ruled in *Guss v. Utah Labor Relations Board* that the states could not assert jurisdiction over private sector labor relations cases unless the NLRB specifically ceded its jurisdiction.[3] Even if the

NLRB ceded its jurisdiction, Section 10(c) of the Taft-Hartley Act requires the state law to be identical to and applied in the same manner as the Taft-Hartley Act. At this time no state law qualified for application to the private sector.

In 1959 Congress passed the Landrum-Griffin Act.[4] Section 14 of this law permitted states to assert jurisdiction over the private sector when a generally applicable collective bargaining statute has been enacted by the state. As Taylor and Witney observe, "State courts and agencies had the authority to take jurisdiction of cases the Board declined. Nothing in the new law required the states to take jurisdiction over these disputes." Theoretically it is possible for states to assert jurisdiction over private sector labor relations matters if enabling legislation exists; however, there has been little legislative activity in this arena. What legislative action has been observed has typically not mixed private sector and public sector jurisdiction.[5] In Massachusetts, however, the Labor Relations Commission charged with the responsibility to administer the public sector collective bargaining law is also authorized by Rules and Regulations to assert jurisdiction over private sector labor relations.[6]

The merits of co-mingling private and public sector labor relations law have been debated for decades. Whether such an approach ignores fundamental differences between private and public employment, the potential clearly exists for such jurisdictional arrangements.

SUMMARY AND CONCLUSIONS

The structure and functions of administrative law agencies are generally modeled after the National Labor Relations Board. The lessons of the New Deal period show that functions and structure are meaningless unless there is a clearly defined relationship between the courts and the agency. The agency must be empowered to seek enforcement of its orders in a court of law; otherwise there is no effective method for the law to be meaningfully applied.

The functions of most boards are similar to those of the National Labor Relations Board. The various states have, however, tailored their statutes to meet their own needs. There have been significant added responsibilities having nothing to do with public sector labor relations. Thus far there are few, if any, examples of legislative actions that bring private sector labor relations under public sector administrative law agencies, even though that is now clearly possible. In California one board is responsible for the administration of several statutes, and the Landrum-Griffin Act (Section 14) permits states to assert jurisdiction in vacated areas of the private sector.

The administrative law agency under any collective bargaining statute has numerous functions that are universally spelled out by statute. The agency is to assure that the law is interpreted and applied to make the parties' respective rights and obligations meaningful so as to assure tranquil and effective labor–management relations.

NOTES

1. Benjamin Taylor and Fred Witney, *Labor Relations Law*, 5th ed. (Englewood Cliffs, N.J.: Prentice-Hall, 1987), 153.

2. Section 3563, Chapter 12, Division 4, Title I, Government Code of the State of California.

3. 353 U.S. 1 (1957).

4. 73 Stat. 519.

5. Taylor and Witney, 256–258.

6. 402 CMR 1.00 Rules and Regulations of the Labor Relations Commission, Section 1.03.

5

Unionization, Organization, and Employee–Employer Rights

Probably no other area of labor law is more controversial or dynamic than employer and employee rights and how those rights are effected by unionization and concerted action. Many individuals hold personal values that are inconsistent with concerted actions by employees and are therefore typically ideologically opposed to unions. Many also believe that employees do not have an equal basis from which to negotiate terms and conditions of employment and are therefore committed to unionization. In any event, this body of law has been, from its beginnings, the subject of debate and controversy.

The applicable law in this arena is divided into two major areas. The U.S. Constitution applies to employees' freedom of association and speech, and therefore shapes some employee rights. Beyond the Constitution are numerous and varied provisions of state collective bargaining laws that assure employees, unions, and employers specific rights in collective bargaining relations. The specification and interactions of these rights form the boundaries of the law herein examined.

The organization of employees, their rights to join unions and engage in concerted action, and the rights of employee organizations and public agencies are the subjects of this chapter. Employee rights to form and join unions are examined before an analysis of employee and union rights under collective bargaining and meet and confer laws is presented. An examination of employer rights under collective bargaining and meet and confer laws is also presented.

EMPLOYEE RIGHTS TO JOIN AND FORM UNIONS

To understand labor law and its role in unionizing campaigns and collective bargaining, one must first understand the motivations of public sector employees in joining and forming unions. A brief discussion of the reasons for employees joining unions is offered before proceeding to a discussion of the law concerning employee unionization rights.

Why People Join and Form Unions

Labor law does not cause unionization; does little except to facilitate or discourage workers in seeking union representation. There is extensive literature examining employee motivations to join and form unions in the private sector. Very little research has been done concerning why public employees join and form unions, but what evidence exists suggests that public employees seek union representation for exactly the same reasons that private sector employees do.[1]

In the private sector employees join and form unions because of "bread and butter" issues. Employee dissatisfaction with terms and conditions of employment, including wages, hours, working conditions, and managerial practices, are the foundations of concerted activity. In other words, employees join unions to improve economic conditions and to gain an effective voice in the workplace. Individually no employee, without unique skills or knowledge valued by an employer, can hope to influence effectively his or her terms and conditions of employment. For the vast majority of employees, influence can be had only through the concerted activities offered by unions, and in this regard public and private sector employees do not differ significantly in their attitudes and reasons for unionization.[2]

Can Public Employees Join Unions?

In the United States state and local government employees have the right to form, join, and assist labor unions, even in the absence of statutory law protecting rights to union membership or activity. The First Amendment assures persons the right of freedom of association. This right was tested as it applied to public employees forming and joining labor unions. Prior to 1968 state courts had generally upheld statutes that proscribed public employees from joining labor organizations. In 1968 the Seventh United States Court of Appeals issued its decision in *McLaughlin v. Tilendis*.[3] Two teachers from Cook County in Illinois were discharged by their employer school district for having associated with Local 1663 of the American Federation of Teachers, and they brought suit for violation of their civil rights under Section 1 of the Civil Rights Act of 1871.[4] The District Court dismissed the suit, holding that the plaintiffs had no First Amendment rights to join or form a labor union. The Seventh Circuit reversed the District Court and remanded the cause for trial. The Appeals Court ruled:

It is settled that teachers have the right of free association, and unjustified interference with teachers; associational freedom violates the Due Process clause of the Fourteenth Amendment. *Shelton v. Tucker*, 364 U.S. 479, 485–487. Public employment may not be subjected to unreasonable conditions, and the assertion of First Amendment rights by teachers will usually not warrant their dismissal . . . Unless there is some illegal intent, an individual's right to form and join a union is protected by the First Amendment.

A state violates the Fourteenth Amendment if it denies public employees their First Amendment rights of freedom of association to form or join a labor union, without a compelling reason to do so. The *McLaughlin* decision, however, simply establishes what the Constitution says. Five years earlier the United States Supreme Court identified the appropriate forum in which to seek a remedy. In *McNeese v. Board of Education* it ruled that a plaintiff need not seek internal or state remedies but may bring suit to protect the right of association directly to the federal courts.[5]

This is not to say that states and cities cannot regulate union membership. In fact, reasonable regulation of association is permissible. In *Perez v. Board of Police Commissioners of the City of Los Angeles* the Court ruled that the city could make reasonable regulations that related to the employees' work and that did not unduly restrict their rights.[6] In this case police officers were barred from joining a union that was not exclusively police officers.

Joining and forming unions are protected, within reasonable limits (compelling interest), even in the absence of protective legislation, but this does not resolve the issue of what those unions can do on behalf of their members.

Union Concerted Actions

McLaughlin settles the issue that public employees may join unions but does not address the issue of what those public employee unions may do in the absence of statutory rights to meet and confer or collectively bargain. In *Smith v. Arkansas State Highway Employees, Local 1315* the Supreme Court ruled that there is nothing in the Constitution that requires a public employer to recognize or to bargain with a public employee union:

Were public employers such as the Commission subject to the same labor laws applicable to private employers, this refusal [to bargain] might well constitute an unfair labor practice. We may assume that it would, and further, that it tends to impair or undermine—if only slightly—the effectiveness of the union in representing the economic interests of its members . . .

But this type of "impairment" is not one that the Constitution prohibits. Far from taking steps to prohibit or discourage union membership or association, all that the Commission has done in its challenged conduct is simply to ignore the union. That it is free to do.[7]

The Constitution protects the freedom of association, but it does not bestow upon unions any rights to collective bargaining nor does it impose any obligation on employers to meet and confer or even recognize the union. If employee organizations are to have legal rights to action, those rights must be created by statute.

State Statutes and Employee Rights

Virtually all meet and confer and collective bargaining laws confirm employee rights to form, join, and support labor unions. At first glance such statutory protections may seem redundant. However, the *McLaughlin* and *Perez* decisions establish only a limited right to join and form unions. It must be remembered that if a government agency has a legitimate and overriding interest, restrictions can be constitutionally imposed on employees' freedom of association.

State collective bargaining statutes that provide employees with broad rights to join and form unions simply eliminate restrictions inherent in the First Amendment guarantees. State statutes also enable employees' unions to engage in specific actions that may not be ignored as the court determined the employer could do in the *Smith* decision. In meet and confer states the rights that unions have is simply to have input into employer decision making and to be informed of employer intentions. Collective bargaining statutes provide for far greater rights.

The majority of state collective bargaining statutes specify employee rights that are very similar to the rights found in Section 7 of the Taft-Hartley Act. For example, the Wisconsin State Employment Labor Relations Act states, in pertinent part:

111.82 Rights of State Employees.—State employees shall have the right of self-organization and the right to form, join or assist labor organizations, to bargain collectively through representatives of their own choosing under this subchapter, and to engage in lawful, concerted activities for the purpose of collective bargaining or other mutual aid or protection. Such employees shall also have the right to refrain from any or all of such activities.[8]

The statutory rights of unions and employees are facilitated by bargaining unit determination and certification procedures and by establishing prohibited (or unfair labor) practices and procedures for enforcement.

Bargaining Unit Determination

Before a certification election can be conducted by an administrative law agency, a bargaining unit must be identified. The Pennsylvania Public Employee Relations Act identifies appropriate bargaining units as:

Sec. 604. [Appropriate Unit.]—The board shall determine the appropriateness of a unit which shall be the public employer unit or a subdivision thereof. In determining the appropriateness of the unit, the board shall:

(1) Take into consideration but shall not be limited to the following: (i) public employees must have an identifiable community of interest, and (ii) the effects of over-fragmentization.

(2) Not decide that any unit is appropriate if such unit includes both professional and nonprofessional employees, unless a majority of such professional employees vote for inclusion in such unit.

(3) Not permit guards at prisons and mental hospitals, employees directly involved with and necessary to the functioning of the courts of this Commonwealth, or any individual employed as a guard to enforce against employees and other persons, rules to protect property of the employer or to protect the safety of persons on the employer's premises to be included in any unit with other public employees, each may form separate homogenous employee organizations with the proviso that organizations of the latter designated employee group may not be affiliated with any other organization representing or including as members, persons outside of the organization's classification.

(4) Take into consideration that when the Commonwealth is the employer, it will be bargaining on a Statewide basis unless issues involve working conditions peculiar to a given governmental employment locale. This section, however, shall not be deemed to prohibit multi-unit bargaining.

(5) Not permit employees at the first level of supervision to be included with any other units of public employees but shall permit them to form their own separate homogenous units. In determining supervisory status the board may take into consideration the extent to which supervisory and nonsupervisory functions are performed.[9]

The law concerning the determination of appropriate bargaining units in Pennsylvania is consistent with the decisions of the National Labor Relations Board and courts in determining what are appropriate bargaining units in the private sector. For example, under paragraph (1) the community of interest and over-fragmentization considerations are concerns addressed by the NLRB in its decision in *Mallinckrodt Chemical Works*.[10] Section 604, paragraph 3 of the Pennsylvania statute handles guards in essentially the same manner as the courts handled plant protection personnel in the private sector.[11] The final paragraph of Section 604 incorporates the NLRB's reasoning in the *Bell Aerospace* decision concerning the organization and representation of supervisory personnel.[12]

Under the Taft-Hartley Act there is no clear definition of bargaining units, only general guidance. It has been left to the NLRB and courts to shape the law governing the proper determination of bargaining units. The drafters of public sector labor laws have again learned from the experience of the private sector and have codified the NLRB and court decisions and included this law as the basis for the expressed statutory language regarding these issues. As one might expect, there are variations from the standards set by the interpretation and application of the Taft-Hartley Act, but there is amazing consistency across the majority of state collective bargaining laws.

Election Policies

The election policies contained in most state statutes are also very similar to those found in the Taft-Hartley Act. Most statutes require at least ten days notice of the time and place of election, secret ballots, that a majority of ballots is necessary to certify a bargaining agent, and that a choice of "no representative" be included on the ballot. These rules and regulations are similar to those found in Taft-Hartley.

Again, the Pennsylvania statute Section 605 (6) states:

The board shall certify the results of said election within five working days after the final tally of votes if no charge is filed by any person alleging that an "unfair practice" existed in connection with said election. If the board has reason to believe that such allegations are valid, it shall set a time for hearing on the matter after due notice. Any such hearing shall be conducted within two weeks of the date of receipt of such charge. If the board determines that the outcome of the election was affected by the "unfair practice" charged or for any other "unfair practice" it may deem existed, it shall require corrective action and order a new election. If the board determines that no unfair practice existed or if it existed, did not affect the outcome of the election, it shall immediately certify the election results.

The election policy language contained in Section 605 (6) incorporates the court's reasoning in the *Gissel*[13] case and *General*

Shoe Doctrine.[14] The Pennsylvania law specifies that one unfair practice is the violation of rules established by the board "regulating the conduct of representation elections."[15] The board rules and regulations list many of the issues concerned in maintaining the laboratory conditions necessary to conduct a certification election. Again, the evidence suggests that Pennsylvania's law is essentially the same as the Taft-Hartley Act. In the majority of state statutes similar language and requirements are also found.

Unfair or Prohibited Practices

Virtually all state collective bargaining statutes enumerate unfair or prohibited practices. Meet and confer statutes do not specify unfair labor practices, except a minority will proscribe interference, restraint, or coercion of employees in joining, forming, or assisting labor organizations.

The majority of collective bargaining statutes specify the same unfair practices listed in the Taft-Hartley Act. The Connecticut State Employee Relations Act states, in pertinent part:

(a) Employers or their representatives or agents are prohibited from: (1) Interfering with, restraining or coercing employees in the exercise of the rights guaranteed in section 5-271 including a look-out; (2) dominating or interfering with the formation, existence or administration of any employee organization; (3) discharging or otherwise discriminating against an employee because he has signed or filed any affidavit, petition or complaint or given any information or testimony under sections 5-270 to 5-280 inclusive; (4) refusing to bargain collectively in good faith with an employee organization, which has been designated in accordance with the provisions of said sections, as the exclusive representative of employees in an appropriate unit; including but not limited to refusing to discuss grievances with such exclusive representative; (5) discriminating in regard to hiring or tenure of employment or any term or condition of employment to encourage or discourage membership in any employee organization; (6) refusing to reduce a collective bargaining agreement to writing and to sign such agreement; (7) violating any of the rules and regulations established by the board regulating the conduct of representation elections.[16]

    As can be readily observed, prohibited practice number 7 under the Connecticut statute is identical to the same paragraph under the Pennsylvania statute. Pennsylvania, however, adds two prohibited practices, concerning the requirements to meet and confer for certain employers and the failure to comply with an arbitrator's award under the statutory impasse procedures. However, the consistency of prohibited practices across states is striking, as is the similarity with the requirements of the Taft-Hartley Act for the protection of unions and employees.

    The prohibited practice sections of state collective bargaining laws are designed to protect the respective rights of the parties. Prohibiting practices that are destructive of the parties' rights and establishing procedures to enforce these provisions are necessary if peaceful collective bargaining is to be fostered and governmental services are to be continued unfettered by strife.

EMPLOYER RIGHTS

    Virtually all collective bargaining and meet and confer statutes specify employer rights. There is statutory identification of specific duties, obligations, and rights for employers. As with employee and union rights, most collective bargaining statutes enumerate unfair or prohibited practices against unions. Further, most statutes also specify the relation of the collective bargaining law with other statutes that effect the public employer. Each of these topics is reviewed in the following paragraphs.

Employer Rights

    A bare majority of state collective bargaining statutes contain language specifically identifying employer rights. The Iowa Public Employment Relations Act states:

Sec. 7. Public Employer Rights—Public employers shall have, in addition to all powers, duties, and rights established by constitutional provision, statute, ordinance, charter, or special act, the exclusive power, duty and the right to:

1. Direct the work of its public employees.

2. Hire, promote, demote, transfer, assign, and retain public employees in positions within the public agency.

3. Suspend or discharge public employees for proper cause.

4. Maintain the efficiency of governmental operations.

5. Relieve public employees from duties because of lack of work or for other legitimate reasons.

6. Determine and implement methods, means, assignments and personnel by which the public employer's operations are to be conducted.

7. Take such actions as may be necessary to carry out the mission of the public employer.

8. Initiate, prepare, certify and administer its budget.

9. Exercise all powers and duties granted to the public employer by law.[17]

There exist some variations in the specific rights enumerated in the employer rights sections of state collective bargaining statutes. The Massachusetts collective bargaining law does not have a section outlining public employer rights. In Massachusetts the legislature relies upon the residual principle: unless rights are specifically granted employees or the unions, they remain the powers of the legislature or the public employer. Iowa's law specifically identifies several rights that are specifically vested in the public employer and notices that rights are reserved to the public employer by other statues and the constitution.

Most public sector collective bargaining contracts will contain a management rights clause. This is also true of most private sector contracts. Contract law requires that the employer retains any rights not specifically granted the union and employees by the agreement or elsewhere by law.[18] In this respect, the identification of public employer rights in either the statute or collective bargaining agreement is probably redundant.

Unfair or Prohibited Practices

Virtually all state statutes specify unfair labor practices that unions commit. The majority of state collective bargaining laws follow the lead of the Taft-Hartley Act and proscribe the same sorts of behavior prohibited in the National Labor Relations Act as amended. It is interesting to note that not all of the proscribed practices offer public employers direct protection. Some provisions are designed to offer employees protection. The standard treatment of unfair labor practices is illustrated by the Pennsylvania Employee Relations Act:

(b) Employee organizations, their agents, or representatives, or public employees are prohibited from:

(1) Restraining or coercing employees in the exercise of the rights guaranteed in Article IV of this act.

(2) Restraining or coercing a public employer in the selection of his representative for the purpose of collective bargaining or the adjustment of grievances.

(3) Refusing to bargain collectively in good faith with a public employer, if they have been designated in accordance with the provisions of this act as the exclusive representative of employees in an appropriate unit.

(4) Violating any of the rules and regulations estaolished by the board regulating the conduct of representation elections.

(5) Refusing to reduce a collective bargaining agreement to writing and sign such agreement.

(6) Calling, instituting, maintaining or conducting a strike or boycott against any public employer or picketing any place of business of a public employer on account of any jurisdictional controversy.

(7) Engaging in, or inducing or encouraging any individual employed by any person to engage in a strike or refusal to handle goods or perform services; or threatening, coercing or restraining any person where an object thereof is to (i) force or require any public employer

to cease dealing or doing business with any other person or (ii) force or require a public employer to recognize for representation purposes an employee organization not certified by the board.

(8) Refusing to comply with the provisions of an arbitration award deemed binding under section 903 of Article IX.

(9) Refusing to comply with the requirements of "meet and discuss."[19]

Again the comparison of the unfair labor practice provisions of the Pennsylvania statute with the Taft-Hartley Act shows significant similarities. The Pennsylvania statute adds sections requiring meet and confer obligations for certain employers and proscribes strike activities, but in most other respects follows the lead of the Taft-Hartley Act.

There are statutes that differ significantly. The Montana Collective Bargaining for Public Employees law identifies only three unfair labor practices of unions: coercion of employees, refusal to bargain in good faith, and using agency shop fees for political contributions.[20]

As was discussed above, the proscription of unfair labor practices is necessary if public employer rights are to be protected. In 1935, the National Labor Relations Act was passed without proscriptions of union practices detrimental to employer rights. It was not until the Taft-Hartley amendment in 1947 that this mistake was corrected and employer rights protected.[21] The Montana statute shows that at a minimum the obligation to bargain in good faith and to refrain from coercing employees in the exercise of their rights is necessary if collective bargaining is to exist. The remaining proscribed practices are necessary to assure the peacefulness and efficiency of bargaining.

Relation of Statutes

Civil service acts have been adopted in a majority of states and municipalities.[22] Since 1971 the courts have consistently ruled that in states with collective bargaining statutes the collective bargaining agreement takes precedence over the state civil service act unless otherwise specified in the collective bargaining law.[23] The civil service acts are, however, an exception. In most other cases other statutes will be given deference by the courts and found to be limiting on collective bargaining.

Several states notice the requirements of various other bodies of law. Almost every state has unique budgeting, financing, or taxing provisions that will impact the timing and nature of negotiations. These financing implications are typically recognized in the notice, good faith bargaining, or impasse provisions of the collective bargaining statutes of the various states.

Even in the absence of specific legislative recognition of the financing and taxing functions of government, such functions are recognized by the Constitution. The Supreme Court issued a landmark decision in 1976 that clearly established the principle that state and local governments are vested with certain powers and must exercise their responsibilities to act for the public welfare.[24] In this regard the government is responsible for taxing and financing. To the extent that the public employer is limited in what it may do with respect to this issue, the employer's constraints must take precedence over collective bargaining considerations. In other words, if mill levies are regulated, then a collective bargaining agreement cannot cause the employer to violate its taxing limits.

In public safety bargaining units it is common for there to exist civilian review boards for disciplinary action involving police officers and firefighters. Unless the collective bargaining statute specifically recognizes the alternative board and vests authority in that entity, the collective bargaining agreement will take precedence over such statutes.[25]

The Iowa Public Employment Relations Act, Section 29, states:

Sec. 28 Inconsistent Statutes—Effect.—A provision of the Code which is inconsistent with any term or condition of a collective bargaining agreement which is made final under the chapter shall supersede the term or condition of the collective bargaining agreement unless otherwise provided by the general assembly.[26]

Where state statutes address the issues of conflicting statutes and the relationship between the collective bargaining law and other statutes, they are typically handled as illustrated by the Iowa law.

SUMMARY AND CONCLUSIONS

Public employees have a constitutional right of freedom of association that extends to membership in labor organizations. This right is limited only by compelling interests of the public employer. The constitutional guarantee, however, does not extend to the recognition of unions or collective bargaining. A public employer is free to ignore employee organizations unless there is law requiring some action.

Most collective bargaining statutes specify employee and union rights. In the majority of such statutes those specified rights will be very similar to those of private employees under the Taft-Hartley Act. Fewer state statutes specify public employer rights.

All collective bargaining statutes specify prohibited or unfair labor practices. In general, the proscribed practices are very similar to the unfair labor practice provisions found in the Taft-Hartley Act. There are additional proscribed practices that are found in several state statutes that deal with issues unique to the public sector. Montana and other states also specify fewer proscribed practices than what is found in the Taft-Hartley Act. Unfair or prohibited practice provisions and mechanisms for their enforcement are what makes the public sector collective bargaining effective; without them the employer and union are free to ignore their respective obligations.

Law that conflicts with state collective bargaining statutes will typically take precedence over collective bargaining. The major exception is that the courts have ruled that civil service acts are superseded by collective bargaining laws. In general, state bargaining laws will remain silent on conflicting laws or specify that contract provisions in conflict with statute are null and void.

There is a broad range of similarity between state statutes concerning employee, employer, and union rights. For the most part, there is remarkable consistency between the majority of state laws and the Taft-Hartley Act. This suggests that state legislatures have learned from private sector experience and have adopted those portions of private sector law that serve their jurisdictions and added and deleted as local conditions warranted.

NOTES

1. For example, see R. L. Smith and A. Hopkins, "Public Employee Attitudes Toward Unions," *Industrial and Labor Relations Review* 32 (1979): 484–495; Jack Stieber, *Public Employee Unionism: Structure, Growth, Policy* (Washington, D.C.: Brookings Institution, 1973); and K. Warner, R. Chisholm, and R. Munzenrider, "Motives for Unionization Among State Social Service Employees," *Public Personnel Management* 7 (1978): 181–191.

2. For further discussion on why private sector employees join unions see Thomas Kochan, "How American Workers View Labor Unions," *Monthly Labor Review* 102 (1979): 90–101.

3. 398 F.2d 287 (1968).

4. 42 U.S.C. para. 1983.

5. 373 U.S. 668 (1963).

6. 178 P.2d 537 (1948).

7. 99 S. Ct. 1826 (1979).

8. Sections 80 through 97, Chapter 111, Subchapter V, Wisconsin Statutes.

9. Public Law 563, No. 195.

10. 162 NLRB 48 (1966).

11. *NLRB v. Atkins & Company.* 331 U.S. 398 (1947).

12. 219 NLRB 384 (1975).

13. *NLRB v. Gissel Packing*, 395 U.S. 575 (1969).

14. The first in a long series of cases concerning the laboratory conditions necessary in which to conduct a certification election, *General Shoe Corporation*, 77 NLRB 124 (1948).

15. Section 1201 (7).

16. (Ct. St. Employees Act)

17. Chapter 20, Code of Iowa.

18. Clarence R. Deitsch and David A. Dilts, *The Arbitration of Rights Disputes in the Public Sector* (Westport, Conn.: Quorum Books, 1990): 75–76.

19. Pennsylvania Public Law 563, No. 195, Section 1201.

20. Title 39, Chapter 31 of the Revised Code of Montana.

21. See Benjamin Taylor and Fred Witney, *Labor Relations Law*, 5th ed. (Englewood Cliffs, N.J.: Prentice-Hall, Inc., 1987), chapters 9 and 10 for further discussion.

22. National Civil Service League, *Survey of Current Personnel Systems in State and Local Governments* (1970), 1–28.

23. *Sloan v. Warren Civil Service Commission*, 192 N.W.2d 499 (1971).

24. *Hortonville Jt. School Dist. No. 1 v. Hortonville Education Association*, 426 U.S. 482 (1976).

25. *Pontiac Police Officers Association v. City of Pontiac*, 94 L.R.R.M. 2175 (1976).

26. Chapter 20, Code of Iowa.

6

The Law and Negotiations

Negotiations are not conducted in a vacuum. The negotiation of a collective bargaining agreement is conducted within the legal, political, and socioeconomic environment in which the respective parties function. Labor law therefore is an important determinant of how negotiations will be conducted and hence the results of the bargaining.

This chapter examines labor law that affects the negotiations of a contract. It first examines the scope of negotiations before examining the obligation to bargain collectively. The scope of bargaining is the setting of bounds over which issues are to be subject to the bargaining process. The obligation to bargain collectively is concerned with several important aspects of law. Included within this area of law are the nature of the bargaining required, good-faith negotiations, and external law considerations.

There is considerable variation across jurisdictions in the status of the law. The scope of negotiations, the obligation to bargain, and the effect of constitutional law and other statutes on the bargaining process differ from state to state. Generalizations are therefore somewhat difficult to make concerning this body of law. There are, however, some useful observations. Several states have statutes that differ very little from the private sector law (Taft-Hartley) concerning both the scope of bargaining and, with the notable exception of strikes, the obligation to bargain. There are several states, however, that specify the scope of bargaining differently from what Congress did in Taft-Hartley.

Add to these complications the fact that the law changes over time, and it becomes apparent that only the general principles of the law can be meaningfully presented. Specific minor variations in law will be ignored here for sake of generality, but significant variations of interest will be examined.

SCOPE OF BARGAINING

Both the Taft-Hartley Act and the Civil Service Reform Act describe the scope of bargaining. The Taft-Hartley Act provides for bargaining to occur concerning "terms and conditions" of employment. The Civil Service Reform Act specifies a "laundry list" of negotiable issues. These two models are significant because they serve as guides for most state collective bargaining laws, with modifications, in many cases, to serve perceived local needs.

Section 8 (d) of the Taft-Hartley states:

For purposes of this section, to bargain collectively is the performance of the mutual obligation of the employer and the representative of the employees to meet at reasonable time and confer in good faith with respect to wages, hours, and other terms and conditions of employment, or the negotiation of an agreement, or any question arising thereunder, and the execution of a written contract incorporating any agreement reached if requested by either party, but such obligation does not compel either party to agree to a proposal or require the making of a concession: Provided, that where there is in effect a collective-bargaining contract covering employees in an industry affecting commerce, the duty to bargain collectively shall also mean that no party to such contract shall terminate or modify such contract, unless the party desiring termination or modification . . .

The Civil Service Reform Act of 1978, Title VII, Subpart F, Subchapter I, Paragraph 7101 (a) (14) states:

"conditions of employment" means personnel policies, practices, and matters, whether established by rule, regulation, or otherwise, affecting working conditions, except such term does not include policies, practices, and matters—

(A) relating to political activities prohibited under subchapter III of chapter 73 of this title;

(B) relating to the classification of any position; or

(C) to the extent such matters are specifically provided for by Federal statute; . . .

Sec. 704 (a) Those terms and conditions of employment and other employment benefits with respect to Government prevailing rate employees to whom section 9(b) of Public Law 92-392 applies which were subject of negotiations in accordance with prevailing rates and practices prior to August 19, 1972, shall be negotiated on and after the date of the enactment of this Act in accordance with the provisions of section 9(b) of Public Law 92-392 without regard to any provision of chapter 71 of title 5, United States Code (as amended by this title), to the extent that any such provision is inconsistent with the paragraph.

(b) The pay and pay practices relating to employees referred to in paragraph (1) of this subsection shall be negotiated in accordance with prevailing rates and pay practices without regard to any provision of—

(A) chapter 71 of title 5, United States Code (as amended by this title), to the extent that any such provision is inconsistent with this paragraph;

(B) subchapter IV of chapter 53 and subchapter V of chapter 55 of title 5, United States Code; or

(C) any rule, regulation, decision, or order relating to rates of pay or pay practices under subchapter IV of chapter 53 of subchapter V of chapter 55 of title 5, United States Code.

As can be seen from the Civil Service Act of 1978, the laundry list is an exclusive listing of items; in other words, terms and conditions of employment are negotiable with specific exceptions. The exceptions include all items within the power of Congress to decide. Some state bargaining statutes, such as New Jersey, use this specific model. Other forms of laundry lists are also in evidence. In Iowa and Kansas for example, specific issues to be bargained are specifically identified in the statutes.

The scope of bargaining generally uses some classification scheme to determine what must be bargained (mandatory issues), may be bargained, if mutually acceptable (permissible issues), and may be bargained (illegal issues). This classification scheme is again borrowed from the interpretation and application of the Taft-Hartley Act.[1]

In general, the mandatory issues of collective bargaining in the public sector are terms and conditions of employment that are not reserved by statute or constitution to be determined in other forums. Permissible issues of collective bargaining are issues that are generally not terms and conditions of employment, but are closely related and may be negotiated if both parties agree and there are no statutory or constitutional prohibitions of such negotiations. Illegal issues are those items specifically proscribed to negotiations by the constitution of the state or statute (either the bargaining law or some other statute).

The effect of laundry lists is to identify specifically the legislative intent in classifying the bargaining issues. The 1978 Civil Service Reform Act identifies issues reserved to the agencies and the Congress and then states that all other issues commonly classified as terms and conditions are mandatory issues of bargaining. In other words, the laundry list identifies illegal issues. In the Kansas Professional Negotiations Act, specific issues are identified that are mandatory issues. If not identified as mandatory, the issue is either permissible or illegal.

Effect of Scope Bargaining

The legal definition of scope of bargaining may dramatically affect the conduct and results of collective bargaining. In jurisdictions where specific issues are precluded as topics of negotiations, the parties may not include them in their contracts. What has occurred in many jurisdictions, however, is that issues closely related that may not otherwise have been critical issues take on substantial importance in negotiations. For example, under the Kansas Professional Negotiations Act teachers and school boards are precluded from negotiations concerning the criteria for teacher evaluations. The procedures to be used in evaluation are bargainable issues. Consequently, the parties focus their negotiations on evaluation procedures and the substantive effect of the procedures on the overall evaluation process. In so doing, teacher unions can have a significant impact on the nature of the evaluations without negotiating over criteria. There are numerous examples of such effects in various jurisdictions.

The limitations of the range of issues available to parties to negotiate has been argued to have an effect on the incidence of impasse. It has been conjectured that if the range of issues is limited, there is less possibility for disagreements that reach the impasse stage. However, the experience of many jurisdictions, such as New York, Iowa, and Kansas, is that economic packages are almost always associated with impasse. If the scope of bargaining includes economic issues, then the scope of bargaining may not appreciably affect impasses. This is an empirical question for which there is not yet a conclusive answer.

OBLIGATION TO BARGAIN

The obligation to bargain has several dimensions. The existence of enabling legislation for collective bargaining will determine whether there is any obligation to bargain. Assuming that state law exists, the statute will typically specify whether the obligation to bargain is to bargain collectively or simply to meet and confer. If collective bargaining is specified, there are specific obligations imposed on both parties by virtually every statute. Each of these issues is examined in the following paragraphs.

Existence of Law

The obligation to bargain is statutory. State courts have ruled rather consistently that in the absence of specific enabling legislation or legal authority, public employers are not obligated to collective bargaining with the representatives of their employees.[2] Where disagreement arises among jurisdictions is whether negotiations can voluntarily occur between an employer and a union in the absence of enabling legislation. In Virginia the courts have ruled that the state had no power to enter into a collective bargaining arrangement in the absence of expressed statutory authority to do so.[3] In Colorado, however, the courts have determined that a school employer may enter into a collective bargaining arrangement with a teachers' union, except that the board is limited to negotiate only over items that are not otherwise limited by statute.[4]

In the absence of state law, several jurisdictions within states have enacted legislation to protect collective bargaining rights. Detroit, New York, and San Francisco have collective bargaining policies and statutes that predate the state collective bargaining laws.[5]

Collective Bargaining Versus
Meet and Confer

State statutes differ in the type of representation employees are authorized. In general, the representation contemplated in state statutes falls into two specific categories, collective bargaining and meet and confer. As discussed earlier, the majority of state statutes require collective bargaining; however, there are state statutes that do not require collective bargaining but only that parties meet and confer.

Meet and confer obligations are far less than those associated with collective bargaining. Collective bargaining statutes require parties to "meet and confer"; however, such statutes also establish other obligations. Collective bargaining statutes require parties to meet and confer to negotiate concerning bargainable items and/or a contract. There are generally unfair labor practices (sometimes called prohibited practices) specified in the statute that require the parties to bargain in good faith. Certain enforcement mechanisms, such as a public employment relations board, put teeth into these requirements in collective bargaining statutes.

Meet and confer statutes typically have no prohibition of bad faith bargaining, nor do they specify that the purpose of the conferring is anything more than an opportunity to share views before management makes the final decision concerning the terms and conditions of employment. There are almost never any specifically prohibited practices nor provisions for any enforcement process. Finally, meet and confer laws do not contemplate the parties negotiating a contract. In fact, all that is contemplated is that management unilaterally retains decision-making authority but must give employees or their representative an opportunity to present their views before the decision is made or implemented. States such as Alabama and Georgia specify meet and confer for public safety employees. Missouri specifies meet and confer for all employees except teachers and police officers, and Texas specifies meet and confer for teachers. Almost all other states that have statutes require collective bargaining (except specific employees in California).[6]

Obligations Under Collective Bargaining Statutes

Collective bargaining statutes impose several obligations on the parties that can be classified into two distinct categories. The first category is threshold issues, those issues concerned with the mechanics and protocol of bargaining. The second category contains issues concerning the conduct of negotiations. Included in this category are issues dealing with the technical aspects of bargaining and the behaviors of the parties.

Threshold Requirements

Consistent with the requirements of Taft-Hartley, most state statutes place certain basic requirements on the parties. The Taft-Hartley Act requires parties to "meet and confer at reasonable times and reasonable places." Most state collective bargaining statutes also require that management negotiate with the exclusive representatives of the employees. That is, the employer may not negotiate with individual employees, but negotiate only with unions concerning current employees' terms and conditions of employment.[7]

There are interesting variants on threshold requirements to be found in several jurisdictions. For example, most state and local collective bargaining agreements are one-year contracts. This results from the public finance principles under which most jurisdictions operate. Iowa, Kansas, Indiana, and several other states place time limits on the parties for the various phases of bargaining. Demands for opening contracts or specific issues are often to be made by the parties at a specific point in the calendar year.

The Kansas Professional Negotiations Act at section 72–5423 states:

Notices to negotiate on new items or to amend an existing contract must be filed on or before December 1 in any school year by either party, such notices shall be in writing and delivered to the superintendent of schools or to the representative of the bargaining unit and shall contain reasonable and understandable detail of the purpose of the new or amended items desired.[8]

Other jurisdictions set deadlines at other places in the negotiations process. Chapter 20 of the Code of Iowa 1990, the Iowa Public Employment Relations Act states in pertinent part:

The negotiations of a proposed collective bargaining agreement by representatives of a state public employer and a state employee organization shall be complete not later than March 15 of the year when the agreement is to be effective . . . [9]

In Iowa the parties are permitted to agree to extend deadlines for the completion of negotiations. The experience of most jurisdictions with legislative action is that set deadlines are not binding upon anyone except the parties to collective bargaining, and state legislatures are frequently tardy in resolving budgetary matters.

Almost every state collective bargaining law has unique provision. This is nowhere more evident than in New York's Taylor Act. Section 204a states:

1. Any written agreement between a public employer and an employee organization determining the terms and conditions of employment of public employees shall contain the following notice in type not smaller than the largest type used elsewhere in such agreement:
"It is agreed by and between the parties that any provision of this agreement requiring legislative action to permit its implementation by amendment of law or by providing the additional funds therefor, shall not become effective until the appropriate legislative body has given approval."

2. Every employee organization submitting such a written agreement to its members for ratification shall publish such notice, include such notice in the documents accompanying such submission and shall read it aloud at any membership meeting called to consider such ratification.

3. Within sixty days after the effective date of this act, a copy of this section shall be furnished by the chief fiscal officer of each public employer to each public employee. Each public employee employed thereafter shall, upon such employment be furnished with a copy of the provisions of this section.[10]

The Taylor Act imposes upon the parties a requirement for specific language to be included within their collective bargaining agreement. The National Labor Relations Board has been reversed by the federal courts for attempting to impose specific contract language on the parties; the courts in New York, however, have not been so disposed.[11]

Most statutes do not require parties to negotiate at specific times, in specific locations, adopt smoking policies for negotiations sessions, and other such groundrules. Most jurisdictions, however, make the establishment of such groundrules for negotiations mandatory issues of collective bargaining. Groundrules are important to the pragmatic establishment of a bargaining relation and as such are governed by the requirement to negotiate in good faith.

Conduct of Negotiations

The parties are universally required to bargain in good faith under collective bargaining statutes. Good faith negotiations are the core of the body of law that concerns the conduct of negotiations. Several state statutes offer specific definitions of good faith bargaining. These definitions are typically of the nature found in the Taft-Hartley Act; that is, to meet and confer with respect to mandatory issues and with an intent to negotiate a contract. Generally the statutes also require the execution of a written contract if either party so demands.

To understand bargaining in good faith requires a review of the private sector law that has been generally adopted in the public sector. The unique complications peculiar to the public sector can then be meaningfully examined.

The basis of the private sector law concerning bargaining in good faith is that the parties enter into negotiations with "an open and fair mind, and a sincere purpose to find a basis of agreement."[12] In other words, the administrative law agency must determine the state of mind of negotiators in determining whether good faith existed during negotiations. Very frequently the administrative law agencies charged with the responsibility to ascertain whether good faith bargaining existed during specific negotiations must rely on circumstantial evidence and inference concerning the outcomes of bargaining. Such records of evidence make generalizations somewhat risky concerning how administrative law agencies rule in such matters.

The National Labor Relations Board and courts have established a set of standards that set the parameters of good faith bargaining. These standards include:[13]

1. There must be a serious attempt to adjust differences and reach an acceptable common ground.

2. Counterproposals must be offered when another party's proposal is rejected. This must involve the "give and take" of an auction system.[14]

3. A position with regard to contract terms may not be constantly changed.[15]

4. Evasive behavior during negotiations is not permitted.[16]

5. There must be a willingness to incorporate oral agreements into a written contract.[17]

These private sector tests of the existence of bargaining in good faith have been utilized by virtually every state administrative law agency under collective bargaining laws.[18]

There are uniquely public sector difficulties in determining whether the parties have bargained in good faith. It is often alleged that the negotiator representing a public employer does not have the authority to commit the employer to bargains reached in negotiations. Negotiators must have the authority to represent their respective constituencies. Collective bargaining implies the authority of negotiators to create obligations which the parties are willing and able to honor.[19] To fail to vest the appropriate authority in selected negotiators will be viewed by administrative law agencies as a failure to bargain in good faith. It should be remembered, however, that where required by law or properly agreed to by the parties, ratification of negotiated contracts and acceptance or rejection of final offers are not violations of this principle of law.[20] Where governing bodies, such as city commissions or other such authorities, cannot delegate their authority over wages, working conditions, or issues of bargaining, these entities may be required to negotiate directly with unions and not appoint agents for such purposes.[21]

In the private sector there must be sharing of information between the parties sufficient to facilitate collective bargaining. For example, if an employer asserts that it cannot meet a wage demand, the employer must support this assertion with proof.[22] There is an interesting complication to this doctrine in the public sector. Most states require that public financial records be made available for public inspection. In such cases, the public employer is not required to provide proof of claims if the information is available to the general public. It is presumed that the union may avail itself of the general right of access to information necessary to negotiate effectively.[23]

In general, public employers bear the same responsibility to refrain from unilateral action that is imposed on private sector employers by the Taft-Hartley Act. There are complications created by the one-year contracts typically negotiated in the public sector. In general, administrative law agencies for the various states have ruled that contract obligations cease with the expiration of the contract, except where expressly provided for by the contract or statute.[24]

In virtually every other respect the interpretation and application of the term *good faith* by state administrative law agencies mirrors the ruling of the NLRB and the federal courts. This uniformity of interpretation should come as no great surprise. Good faith is a necessary prerequisite to effective and peaceful negotiations, which is generally the stated purpose of state collective bargaining statutes. The public policy of states not desiring to establish the requirements of good faith delineated by the NLRB have opted for meet and confer or no legislation whatsoever. Because of the relatively late adoption of collective bargaining statutes in state and local jurisdictions, legislators had the advantage of having the developed body of private sector law to guide their creation of policy. The timing of the development of public sector bargaining therefore did not require the reinvention of good faith bargaining.

EXTERNAL LAW

The role of external law in the arbitration of labor disputes, contract negotiations, and contract administration is of little relevance in the private sector. The Civil Rights Act of 1964, Fair Labor Standards Act, and other regulatory statutes simply guarantee minimum employee rights and therefore impose few restrictions on the parties' negotiations. If anything in the private sector, unions benefit by not risking, at the bargaining table, certain minimum employment standards that are fixed by regulatory statutes. In the public sector, however, external law imposes significant constraints on the parties' negotiations. The external law constraints effect both the scope of bargaining and what constitutes bargaining in good faith.

The external law constraints on public sector collective bargaining are of two varieties: constitutional constraints and statutory constraints other than those found in the collective bargaining statute.

Constitutional Constraints

The First Amendment, as previously discussed, protects public employees' rights to form and join labor organizations and unions in the absence of statutory protections. The Constitution, however, does not compel public employers to negotiate with public employee unions.[25] Beyond this threshold constitutional issue concerning bargaining relations, several state constitutions limit the authority of legislative bodies to delegate authority. School boards, city commissions, and county commissions are often vested with powers they must themselves fulfill. Such constitutional prohibitions of delegations of authority serve to remove issues from collective bargaining in jurisdictions where bargaining statutes exist.

State constitutions also may limit the scope of bargaining in other ways. Most states that have enacted prohibitions of union security clauses (so-called right-to-work laws) have done so through statutory means. In Kansas, however, the prohibition of union security clauses was done through constitutional a-mendment. In Kansas, therefore, union security clauses are illegal issues of collective bargaining for both private and public bargaining relations.

Statutory Constraints

State statutes concerning financing, education, personnel administration, and regulatory issues effect the scope of negotiations and the obligation to bargain. State statutes also will frequently determine the conduct of negotiations.

State budgetary and taxation statutes generally specify financing authority for periods of a single year. The most obvious result of these statutes is that the preponderance of collective bargaining agreements in the public sector are for one year. By contrast, most private sector collective bargaining agreements are multiyear contracts, generally of three years duration. Without the need to have taxing and budgeting authority annually renewed, private sector entities can avoid the limitation on the duration of their contracts imposed by law.

Budget and tax authority also place restrictions on how an employer may raise revenue to meet obligations. The result of these statutory regulations is to create often severe constraints on public employers in effectively compensating employees. In the mid-1980s, the farm crisis caused severe limitations on Iowa public employers' abilities to raise revenues. Iowa law limited the mill levy that jurisdictions could impose. Coupled with rapidly declining property values, many jurisdictions found their tax rates virtually fixed with declining tax bases. The end result was that these jurisdictions faced declining budgets with a rising cost of living for their employees. This resulted in bargaining impasses, hard feelings, and inability to compete in labor markets in several jurisdictions.

Noneconomic issues are also often effected by statutes that limit public employers' abilities to bargain. In education, for example, numerous statutes specify various aspects of the terms and conditions of employment. Evaluation criteria, pension plans, school years, length of school day, and curriculum are often specified by statute. When statutory requirements exist, the employer's minimum standards of performance are set without threat from negotiations. On the other hand, public employers may also be constrained to make expenditures that, if they were free to choose, might have significant opportunity costs that would otherwise have resulted in other allocations of resources.

The effect of external law is almost universally recognized by state collective bargaining statutes. As in the case of the 1978 Civil Service Reform Act, most states limit the application of the bargaining statute to be in compliance with requirements of existing statutes (as they may be subsequently amended) concerning employer rights and obligations to the public.

SUMMARY AND CONCLUSIONS

With few exceptions the obligations of public sector unions and employers to bargain in good faith are identical to those found in private employment covered by the Taft-Hartley Act. The scope of bargaining in the public sector may be either a laundry list of items or the terms and conditions of employment. The scope of public sector bargaining is also significantly limited by external law that may either fix certain aspects of employment or limit the employer's ability to delegate authority.

The effects of the law on negotiations is to impose more-restrictive limits on the scope of bargaining than is normally observed in the private sector. The major effect of external law is to restrict further the scope of bargaining in the public sector and generally to limit public sector collective bargaining contracts to one-year durations. Few other directly observable differences in the nature of negotiations can be observed between the public and private sector that are directly attributable to the law concerning the parties' duty to bargain.

NOTES

1. *NLRB v. Wooster Division, Borg-Warner Corp.* 356 U.S. 342 (1958).

2. For example, see *International Union of Operating Engineers, Local 321 v. Water Works Board of the City of Birmingham.* 276 Ala. 462 (1964); and *Dade County v. Amalgamated Association of Street Electric Railway and Motor Coach Employees of America,* 157 So. 2d 176 (1963).

3. *Virginia v. Arlington County,* 232 S.E.2d 30 (1977).

4. *Littleton Education Association v. Arapahoe County School District No. 6.* 533 P.2d 793 (1976).

5. Benjamin Taylor and Fred Witney, *Labor Relations Law,* 5th ed. (Englewood Cliffs, N.J.: Prentice-Hall, 1987), 641.

6. See *Hearings before the Subcommittee on Labor of the Committee on Labor and Human Resources,* United States Senate, Reviewing Practices and Operations under the National Labor Relations Act, January 29, February 5, 1988 (Washington, D.C.: U.S. Government Printing Office, 1988), 151–163.

7. There are exceptions to this basic rule. Under the Kansas Professional Negotiations Act, employers are permitted to negotiate within narrow limits with individual employees if impasse procedures fail to result in a negotiated collective bargaining agreement.

8. Kansas Statutes Annotated 72–5413 et. seq.

9. Code of Iowa 1990, Chapter 20, Section 17, paragraph 10.

10. Chapter 392, L. 1967 as amended.

11. *National Union of Marine Cooks & Stewards v. NLRB,* 90 NLRB 1099 (1950).

12. *Globe Cotton Mills v. NLRB,* 103 F.2d 91, 94 (1939).

13. See Taylor and Witney, Chapter 14, for further discussion.

14. *Majure Transport Company v. NLRB,* 198 F.2d 735 (1952).

15. *NLRB v. Norfolk Shipbuilding & Drydock Corporation.* 172 F.2d 813 (1949).

16. *Na-Mac Product Corporation,* 70 NLRB 298 (1946).

17. *Southern Saddlery Company,* 90 NLRB 1205 (1950).

18. Charles J. Coleman, *Managing Labor Relations in the Public Sector* (San Francisco: Jossey-Bass, 1990), 99–100.

19. *City of Saginaw.* Michigan Employment Relations Commission, 1969 MERC Lab. Op. 293.

20. *City of Detroit*. Michigan Employment Relations Commission, 1970 MERC Lab. Op. 953.

21. *Nation v. State of Wyoming ex rel. Fire Fighters Local 279.* 518 P.2d 931 (1974).

22. *NLRB v. Truitt Manufacturing Company,* 351 U.S. 149 (1956); *Sergeant Bluff-Luton Community School Dist.* Case No. 984 (Iowa PERB 1977); and *Macomb County Community College* (Michigan) 1972 MERC Lab. Op. 775.

23. *Saginaw Township Board of Education.* (Michigan) 1970 MERC Lab. Op. 127.

24. See for example, *Vermont State Employees Association v. State of Vermont,* 92 L.R.R.M. 2309 (1976), and *Ledyard Board of Education.* Decision No. 1564, Conn. St. Bd. Lab. Rel. (1977).

25. *Alaniz v. City of San Antonio* (Texas). 80 L.R.R.M. 2983.

7

Impasse Procedures

This chapter examines the law concerning impasses in public sector bargaining and the procedures specified by law for the resolution of such disputes. The first section examines impasses, the second section deals with the difference between compulsory and voluntary impasse resolution mechanisms, the third section is concerned with "typical" impasse procedures, and the final section presents a discussion of the law concerning court enforcement of interest arbitration awards.

BARGAINING IMPASSES IN THE PUBLIC SECTOR

Impasse resolution procedures have been promulgated in most states to provide a mechanism for labor and management to resolve disputes that arise during contract negotiations. The public sector, in particular, has been the proving grounds for impasse procedures because of the almost general prohibition of strikes and lockouts. The test of economic strength inherent in strikes or lockouts is how most contract disputes are settled in the private sector, but this resort to economic warfare is considered by most policymakers as inconsistent with the role of government. The result is that for many years collective bargaining in the public sector was also regarded as inconsistent with effective government. As attitudes changed, so did public policy, and public employees in most jurisdictions now have rights to unionization and collective bargaining fully protected by statute. The problem then becomes one of how the process of collective bargaining can be made to work if the strike, the traditional means of settling industrial disputes, is not going to be permitted. A substitute for the strike was needed to make the collective bargaining process work in the public sector while providing for the continued delivery of essential public services.

The alternative to the strike, in the absence of impasse procedures, is that management be given the unilateral authority to set wages and other terms and conditions of employment or that authority be entrusted to the legislative branch of government. In either case, the public employee is left without an effective input into terms and conditions of employment. This is a situation that over the past few decades of this century became increasingly intolerable to public employees who wished to have the same or similar rights as those workers in the private sector who had collective bargaining and federal statutes that protected their rights to belong to labor organizations for purposes of concerted representational activities.

The preponderance of states having collective bargaining statutes specify statutory impasse procedures, but these are no better than their enforcement mechanisms. Those states that have final and binding arbitration or permit strikes find that collective bargaining provides an effective method whereby public employees can gain voice concerning their working conditions and the terms for which they exchange their labor. Those states that make no provisions for closure, either through arbitration or strikes, leave public employees with little effective method to influence terms and conditions of employment.

IMPASSE PROCEDURES: VOLUNTARY OR COMPULSORY

The majority of states that have enacted collective bargaining laws have also imposed compulsory impasse procedures. Compulsory impasse procedures are those that must be followed in the cases where the parties have either declared (either jointly or separately) that an impasse exists or have failed to achieve a negotiated settlement of the contract by some specified time. The parties have no choice as to whether or not the impasse resolution procedures will be implemented in the case of compulsory procedures. As a matter of practice or explicitly stated in some statutes, parties at impasse may extend the deadline for declaring an impasse if it appears that they can successfully negotiate their contract.

Several jurisdictions allow parties to negotiate mutually acceptable or voluntary impasse resolution procedures to be used as a substitute for the compulsory procedures identified in the law. The Ohio General Assembly enacted the Public Sector Labor Act in 1983.[1] This law contains several alternative impasse resolution procedures. Under Chapter 4117.13 of the statute, public safety employees, the employees of the state school for the deaf, the state school for the blind, and similar employees are denied the right to strike and must utilize the impasse procedures contained in the statute. All other employees may strike or the impasse may be submitted to the impasse procedures for settlement. In the case of public safety and similar employees, impasse resolution procedures are compulsory, but for all other state employees impasse procedures are voluntary.

It is also interesting to note that the Ohio Act provides for numerous alternatives in the dispute settlement arena. This may be referred to as an arsenal approach to impasse resolution. The Act specifies that:

Sec. 4117.13 (C) In the event the parties are unable to reach an agreement, they may submit, at any time prior to forty-five days before the expiration date of the collective bargaining agreement, the issues in dispute to any mutually agreed upon dispute settlement procedure which supersedes the procedures contained in this section.

(1) The procedures may include:

(a) Conventional arbitration of all unsettled issues;

(b) Arbitration confined to a choice of the last offer of each party to the agreement as a single package;

(c) Arbitration confined to a choice of the last offer of each party to the agreement on each issue submitted;

(d) The procedures described in division (C)(1)(a), (b), or (c) of this subsection and including among the choices for the arbitrator, the recommendations of the fact finder, if there are recommendations, either as a single package or on each issue submitted;

(e) Settlement by a citizens' conciliation council composed of three residents within the jurisdiction of the public employer. The public employer shall select one member and the exclusive representative shall select one member. The two members selected shall select the third member who shall chair the council. If the two members cannot agree upon a third member within five days after their appointments, the Board shall appoint the third member. Once appointed, the council shall make a final settlement of the issues submitted to it pursuant to division (G) of this section.

(f) Any other dispute settlement procedure mutually agreed to by the parties.

The Ohio Act also specifies the more traditional process of mediation, fact finding, and interest arbitration should the parties fail to make a selection under the provisions of Sec. 4117.13 (C) (1). This array of impasse resolution procedures is rather uncommon in most state statutes.

The Ohio statute is rather liberal. On the other hand, Indiana permits collective bargaining for educational employees; however, impasse procedures end up fact finding, and employees are denied the right to strike. This is similar to both bargaining statutes in Kansas. Iowa has a tri-offer arbitration system, and the parties are permitted to skip the fact finding process and convert the tri-offer system into final offer arbitration. Under the tri-offer scheme, the arbitrator is limited to select the final offer of one of the parties or award the fact finder's recommendations. If the parties agree to skip the fact finding step, the arbitrator is left with only the final offers of the parties. Iowa's system therefore contains elements of both a voluntary and a compulsory impasse resolution procedure.

The voluntary or compulsory nature of the impasse resolution procedures used in the public sector is of some significance. State legislatures cannot possibly anticipate the various needs of all the public employers and unions within their jurisdiction. To specify one uniform impasse resolution system that all unions and employers must follow is to assume away the possibility that unique impasse procedures may be more serviceable for specific bargaining relations. States such as Ohio, California, and Iowa that allow some discretion by the parties in selecting the impasse resolution mechanism to be utilized are recognizing that there are individual differences in the bargaining relations and environments within their states. The result of these arsenal approaches to impasse resolution should be more useful and effective impasse resolution procedures.

IMPASSE RESOLUTION PROCEDURES: THE TYPICAL STRUCTURES

There is no uniformly structured impasse procedure. States vary substantially in the steps and the form of procedures utilized. Ohio allows certain employees to strike while mandating that certain other employees use a negotiated procedure or the multistep procedure provided for by the General Assembly. Oregon also provides for compulsory arbitration of contract disputes but limits that interest arbitration to employees who do not have the right to strike.[2] Other states such as Michigan provide for a mediation-arbitration process in which the arbitrator is to act as mediator in carrying out his or her role, but then if an arbitration award becomes necessary, the arbitrator is to select from the final offers of the parties.[3]

The majority of states with impasse procedures make fact finding the final step in statutory impasse procedures.[4] This category includes states such as Indiana and Kansas. Several of these states (fourteen) also allow parties to submit their impasse to arbitration if fact finding fails to resolve the impasse.[5] This category includes states (such as Rhode Island) on issues such as wages that make the remaining issues subject to final and binding arbitration, and Connecticut for employees covered under the Municipal Employee Relations Act of 1965.[6] There are almost as many forms of impasse procedures as there are states.

There are, however, two basic forms of impasse procedures with variations on each theme. These impasse procedures may be classified into two distinct categories, closed-ended and open-ended. A closed-ended impasse procedure is typically a multiple-step procedure frequently beginning with mediation, but all have a definite closure, hence the term closed ended. These procedures typically end in final and binding arbitration or the right of the union to strike or the public employer to lock out. Open-ended impasse procedures are the more common procedures and typically begin with mediation but do not have closure to the process. An open-ended procedure will typically end the dispute settlement process with fact finding. If the parties are unable to resolve the impasse on the basis of the fact finder's report, one of several alternatives is possible. In the case of Kansas, for example, if the parties are unable to resolve their dispute after receipt of the fact finder's report, the public employer is free to issue the terms and conditions of employment provided that such a "unilateral contract" takes into consideration the interests of the public, the agency, and the public employees.

Mediation is almost always the starting point for statutory impasse procedures. Mediation is that form of dispute resolution that is the least intrusive. A mediator is an expert in negotiations and is neutral. The mediator's role is simply that of assisting the parties in reaching a privately negotiated settlement through skills as an intermediary or even as a bargaining consultant.

Fact finding typically follows mediation in most impasse procedures. Fact finding is a quasi-judicial form of impasse settlement in which the fact finder conducts a hearing, gathers the relevant facts, and listens to the parties' respective contentions. After the parties have presented their evidence and made their contentions, the fact finder then adjourns and prepares a written report that typically contains recommendations for resolving the dispute supported by written opinions explaining why the recommendations are fair and should be adopted. The fact finder's report is purely advisory and is effective only if the parties choose to accept the fact finder's recommendations.

Interest arbitration is typically the final step in closed-ended impasse procedures. Interest arbitration is also a quasi-judicial form of dispute resolution and is very similar to fact finding in that a hearing is typically conducted and the arbitrator provides each party with an opportunity to present evidence and contentions. The main difference between fact finding and interest arbitration is that the arbitrator prepares a written award that contains the final and binding resolution of the issues at impasse rather than simply recommendations as to how the parties may be able to negotiate a settlement.

Mediators are generally full-time employees of either the Federal Mediation and Conciliation Service or some counterpart in state government. Mediators are selected for personal characteristics, professional background, and aptitude. Most mediators are then subjected to an extensive training program. Arbitrators and fact finders have two hurdles to clear. The first is panel acceptability, and the second and more rigorous one is party acceptability. Arbitrators are selected either on an ad hoc basis or as permanent umpires for the life of a contract or some other specified time. The real test of whether someone is going to make it as a professional arbitrator or fact finder is whether that person can establish a reputation for excellence with the parties.

ENFORCEMENT OF
INTEREST ARBITRATION AWARDS

In the absence of strikes, impasses that arise during contract negotiations must be settled through alternative dispute resolution mechanisms. Both mediation and fact finding are methods that are dependent upon persuasion; there is no outcome that can be enforced, only recommendations.

The impasse mechanisms are no more effective than procedures available to enforce arbitration awards. There are two methods commonly employed in enforcing interest arbitration awards, prohibited practice litigation and suit for enforcement of the award through the courts, and both will be examined in the following paragraphs.

Unfair or Prohibited Practices

Minnesota[7] and Pennsylvania,[8] for example, make it an unfair labor practice for either party to fail to comply with the award of an arbitrator issued pursuant to statutory impasse procedures. In these states and several others with like proscriptions, the administrative law agency is charged with the authority of investigating the complaint and holding a hearing; if a respondent failed to comply with an award, an order is issued that can be enforced with an injunction.

Massachusetts does not make failure to abide by an arbitrator's award a prohibited practice. Alternatively, Massachusetts proscribes failing to participate in impasse procedures, including mediation, fact finding, and arbitration, in good faith.[9] In *Marlborough Firefighters, Local 1714* the Massachusetts court determined it was appropriate to determine whether the arbitrator's award was in compliance with the statute.[10] In *Local 66, Boston Teachers Union v. School Commission of Boston* the court ruled that enforcement of a collective bargaining agreement, even if created through interest arbitration, is through the grievance and rights arbitration process.[11]

The use of unfair labor practice machinery to enforce interest arbitration awards reduces the time and expense necessary to bring closure to contract disputes. Closely related to the unfair labor practice route is the resolving of such disputes through the grievance procedure and ultimately through rights arbitration, also enforceable through an equity court, as specified in Massachusetts.

Suits in Court

Without unfair labor practices or grievance procedures to enforce interest arbitration awards, parties are left with suit in a court of competent jurisdiction. There is not judicial consensus concerning interest arbitration. In Utah,[12] South Dakota,[13] and Colorado,[14] courts have found that interest arbitration is an unconstitutional delegation of authority from the public employer to an arbitrator. At the time of these decisions, in the mid-1970s, there was no public policy of collective bargaining.

In states with collective bargaining as the state's public policy, interest arbitration has been treated more favorably. Voluntary interest arbitration has been dealt with in the same manner as rights arbitration. Where interest arbitration is not only binding but also compulsory, the courts have exhibited qualified support.

In New Jersey,[15] Washington,[16] and several other states, the courts have consistently ruled that where there is legislative intent for arbitrators to settle labor disputes and there are recognized safeguards to assure that arbitrators stay within the legislative intent of the law, interest arbitration awards will be enforced in the courts.

SUMMARY AND CONCLUSIONS

Impasse resolution procedures are substitutes for the strike and lockout, which are generally prohibited in the public sector. Impasse procedures can be classified in several ways. There are compulsory and voluntary impasse procedures, the former being specified by statute and the latter left to the parties to negotiate a mutually acceptable mechanism. Impasse procedures can also be classified as open ended or closed ended. Open-ended impasse procedures do not provide closure to the bargaining process and typically end with fact finding. If the fact finding recommendation does not provide an acceptable solution, then generally the public employer may take unilateral action of some sort. Closed-ended impasse procedures generally provide some closure to the procedures. The closure is generally either final and binding interest arbitration, or in some cases it permits the union to strike and the public employer to lock out.

The typical impasse procedure provides for mediation and, should this fail, fact finding. The majority of impasse procedures do not require final and binding arbitration, nor do they permit strikes or lockouts. In fourteen states, final and binding arbitration is permitted if mutually acceptable to the parties, but it is not compulsory.

Mediation and fact finding rely on the persuasion of the neutral to be effective. Interest arbitration, however, is effective because the awards can be enforced. Courts in states with collective bargaining statutes typically will enforce an arbitration award where there are appropriate safeguards to assure that neutrals stay within the legislative intent in fashioning their awards. Some states also specify that interest arbitration awards can be enforced through the unfair labor practice procedures contained in the collective bargaining statute.

NOTES

1. Chapter 4117 of the Revised Code of Ohio.
2. See Benjamin Taylor and Fred Witney, *Labor Relations Law*, 4th edition (Englewood Cliffs, N.J.: Prentice-Hall, 1983), Chapter 21 for further discussion.
3. Ibid.
4. Paul D. Standohar, "Constitutionality of Compulsory Arbitration Statutes in Public Employment," *Labor Law Journal* 27, no. 11 (November 1976): 675.
5. Robert E. Dunham, "Interest Arbitration in Non-Federal Public Employment," *Arbitration Journal* 31, no. 1 (March 1976): 45–46.
6. Ibid.
7. Public Employment Relations Act, Section 179.68.

8. Public Employee Relations Act, Public Law 563, No. 195, Section 1201.

9. Section 10, Chapter 150E, General Laws of Massachusetts.

10. *Marlborough Firefighters, Local 1714 v. City of Marlborough*, 378 N.E.2d 437 (1978).

11. 363 N.E. 2d 4924 (1975).

12. *Salt Lake City v. International Association of Firefighters*, 556 P.2d 786 (1977).

13. *City of Sioux Falls v. Sioux Falls Firefighters' Local 814*, 234 N.W.2d 35 (1975).

14. *Greeley Police Union v. City Council*, 553 P.2d 790 (1976).

15. *Division 540, Amalgamated Transit Union v. Mercer County Improvement Authority*, 386 A.2d 1290 (1978).

16. *Spokane v. Spokane Police Guild*, 553 P.2d 1316 (1976).

8

The Effects of
Law on Collective Bargaining

As noted earlier, labor law is an important environmental influence on collective bargaining. Certain aspects of the law dramatically affect the results of negotiations between the parties.

It is very important to note that while the structure influences the likelihood of particular outcomes in bargaining, it does not predetermine what will happen in any individual bargaining relationship. The parties themselves maintain ultimate control over the actual outcome within the limits established by law.

The first major section of this chapter deals with the factors that influence the likelihood of an impasse in negotiations. The interrelationship of influential factors and resolution procedures is discussed at some length.

The second section deals with labor peace. Labor relations statutes generally state explicitly that labor peace is one of the dominant goals of the legislation. Have statutory impasse resolution procedures eliminated strikes in the public sector? No, they have not. The interrelationship of impasse procedures and actual labor peace experience is described. There is more to the issue of labor peace than the strike experiences of a jurisdiction. The continuing labor relationships following resolution of an impasse are issues of very real concern.

What happens to the bargaining relationship when the parties have reached impasse? Clearly it continues just as the chapter continues with a discussion of life after impasse—more precisely, a discussion of what having resorted to impasse means for the negotiating parties and their continuing relationship. The fact finding report and interest arbitration award each complete a step in impasse resolution procedures, but they do not complete the labor relations process. This section guides the practitioner in continuing with that process.

The third section addresses the issue of the bargained outcome vis-à-vis the arbitration outcome. Are bargainers better off with an arbitration award or a negotiated settlement? The authors' strong bias toward contracts that reflect the desires of the parties rather than the judgment of the neutral is supported by evidence cited in this section. Neutrals perform their function well, but they cannot outperform parties intent on reaching an accord.

The fourth section of this chapter addresses the evolution of labor–management cooperation. Many lessons have been learned from successful negotiations, from negotiations resolved after resort to impasse proceedings, and from negotiations that terminated in labor "warfare"—strikes, job actions, and lockouts. The evolution of labor–management cooperation is presented so that novice practitioners learn from the experiences of the past without having to repeat them.

FACTORS AFFECTING IMPASSE AND ITS RESOLUTION

Nothing increases the likelihood of a negotiated settlement (avoiding impasse) more than good faith bargaining. Good faith is descriptive of both behavior and attitude. Both good faith behavior and good faith bargaining are continuums rather than yes/no descriptors. Because behavior is observable and attitude is not, administrative law agencies and courts must infer attitude from behavior. Good faith behavior, at a minimum, means a willingness to meet at reasonable times and places, to negotiate mandatory issues, and to commit agreed upon items to a written contract. This behavior will normally be sufficient to avoid an unfair labor practice conviction.

But the good faith envisaged by most legislatures is something more; it is an attitude of good faith. It calls for an honest attempt by parties to find mutually acceptable terms and conditions of employment, a real desire to negotiate a contract that both parties can live with. It means that the parties enter negotiations with the hopes of ending with a contract. It means that both hope to be able to reach an agreement without third-party intervention. It means that the parties are willing to make full use of third-party assistance, when necessary, to help reach an agreement.

What can one party do when the other is not bargaining in good faith? If the other party does not exhibit good faith bargaining conduct but has a good faith attitude, the conduct is probably due to ignorance, and mediation is likely to be successful. Empirical studies have confirmed the expectation that mediation is most helpful when negotiators are inexperienced.[1] If the other party lacks good faith, little can be done without substantial evidence of bad faith behavior prior to the final step in the resolution procedure. Mediation will likely be ineffective.[2]

Bargaining Stances Based on Principle

Positions taken in negotiations based on a deeply held belief are unlikely to be modified in response to another party's differences in belief. For example, the union negotiator may feel that punching a time clock is demeaning, that bargaining unit members should not have to punch in if management personnel do not have to. Management may see nothing demeaning about using a time clock. Each is likely to find the other's arguments unpersuasive. Such positions based on principle (or strongly felt perceptions) are unlikely to be modified or compromised (double entendre intentional).

Therefore, issues based on principle are likely to lead to impasse. However, this kind of issue is one that mediation has a good chance of resolving.[3] Mediators are adept at helping each party better understand the other's point of view, at helping identify alternatives, and at bringing the discussion back to being issues-oriented rather than feelings-oriented.

Bargaining in "Good Faith" toward Impasse

Good faith includes an attempt to reach contract settlement. Due to the political nature of management and union positions, negotiators may feel too politically threatened to reach settlement without impasse despite a personal desire to settle earlier. Constituents—influential management or union folks—may be insisting on a "hard line" approach in bargaining. Mediation is unlikely to settle such an impasse.

Fact-finding, because of its generally public nature, stands a far better chance of leading to impasse resolution. Parties may be able to blame the fact-finder for concessions they were already prepared to yield. If "hard line" pressures continue, arbitration may be required to settle the dispute. Thomas A. Kochan references the empirical work of James Stern in stating that "management representatives might find the arbitrator to be a useful scapegoat for the adverse public reaction that is likely to result from higher cost settlements."[4]

Hopefully, the party facing political imperatives has given enough clues to the counterpart in negotiations that the political necessities are understood. Though the bargaining process clearly suffers from the lack of a negotiated settlement if the issues go to arbitration, the bargaining relationship may survive the current round of negotiations relatively unscathed. There is no alternative for the negotiator when faced with this bargaining stance but to accept the reality that the impasse is going to fact finding and perhaps arbitration.

A History of Previous Impasses

As statuatory impasse resolution procedures are characteristic of public sector collective bargaining legislation, one concern of proponents is on a possible side effect of the legislation. The concern is that ready access to impasse resolution procedures might cause parties to be less vigorous in their efforts to achieve a voluntary settlement without resorting to third-party intervention. A related concern voiced by the prestigious Taylor Committee is that "dispute settlement procedures can become habit-forming and negotiations become only a ritual."[5] These concerns are collectively called the "narcotic effect" of impasse resolution procedures. One way to determine whether or not a narcotic effect really exists is to examine bargaining histories, comparing the periods before and after impasse procedure resolution were legislated for public employees. A strong narcotic effect was uncovered in a statistically thorough examination of New York police, firefighters, and teachers.[6]

So resort to impasse resolution procedures tends to cause repeated use. Why? Probably because it is easier than doing everything that can be done to prepare for and conduct healthy negotiations. Do parties eventually realize that letting neutrals resolve disputes is not as good as negotiating a settlement themselves? Yes, but it takes some time for the parties to come to that realization, and the evidence as to how long it takes is mixed. Whether the narcotic effect generally lasts for decades or for only a few years remains a matter of debate.[7]

It is important for the practitioners of collective negotiations to strive for mutually determined contract terms. A contract determined by an outsider, even by the most adept of neutrals, is likely to be inferior to a contract negotiated by two parties intent on reaching an accord.

The Structure of
Legislated Impasse Procedures

The New York State study focused on a change in the col-

lective bargaining law that applied to most jurisdictions outside
New York City. The new law added arbitration as a final
step in legislated impasse procedures.[8] The executive branch
(and others presumably) were concerned that increasing the
number of impasse procedure steps would increase resort to
those procedures. The concern proved valid.[9] The New York
State study did show a 16 percent increase in impasse and a 15
percent increase in impasses that went to the final step of impasse
procedures due to the change.[10] However, this effect was partially
offset by an increase in settlements at the mediation step.[11]

The increased success of the initial step (mediation) and
increased resort to the final step (arbitration) focused some
attention on the intermediate step (fact finding). The study reports
that parties took more extreme, inflexible positions on moving to
the fact finding step than they held in earlier negotiations. That
effect was so pronounced that the study recommended elimination
of the fact finding step. Costs and time delays associated with fact
finding were considered to be more burdensome than the limited
benefits fact finding warranted. This appraisal was bolstered by
the similarity between fact finding reports and final arbitration
awards.[12]

Interestingly enough, an Iowa study came to a different conclusion. Gallagher and Pegnetter found that fact finding settled
many disputes without resort to arbitration. The Iowa procedures
in arbitration allowed the neutral to choose either of the parties'
final offer or the fact finder's recommendation. This seemed to
narrow the difference between the parties' final offers: that is,
even when fact finding did not result in a negotiated settlement,
it narrowed the differences between the parties.[13]

Does a set of statuatory impasse resolution procedures generally effect changes in the behavior of bargaining parties? Yes!
Just as expanding a highway will increase its use, expanding
resolution procedures will increase their use. Does this mean
there was no need for the new highway lanes or the new
resolution procedures? No, it does not. The message is that
there is no panacea—no absolute cure for the difficulties that

arise in collective bargaining.

For the practitioner, the change in impasse resolution procedures changes incentives facing each of the bargaining parties. Nonetheless, a mutual attitude of good faith and an understanding of the bargaining process will normally result in successful negotiation of a collective bargaining agreement. Hopefully, the agreement is reached before resort to impasse procedures is required. When that is not the case, an understanding of the process greatly improves the chances of its success in providing a negotiated settlement.

LIFE AFTER IMPASSE

Most labor legislation has explicitly listed labor peace as a primary purpose of the legislation. Labor peace is usually defined as the absence of industrial warfare; it usually means no strikes, work slowdowns, or sickouts.

A study of Indiana teacher unionization is instructive. The Indiana legislature established mandatory mediation and fact finding steps following impasse. It further allowed the parties to agree to interest arbitration to resolve a continuing impasse. There is no observable difference in strike activity between the prelaw and postlaw periods. The statutory impasse procedures had no noticeable impact on strike activity. But it should be noted that the strike activity averaged one school day lost for each school district once every seventeen years![14] While other states experience more public sector strike activity than this, states that prohibit strikes generally do not experience many strikes.

The New Jersey experience surrounded consideration of alternative modifications to an existing state law. "Although most unions publicly advocated the right to strike, many labor leaders privately indicated . . . that they 'would get clobbered' in a strike."[15] In lieu of adopting a right to strike, New Jersey adopted compulsory arbitration of interest disputes. During the next few years there were no strikes over interest issues, though some stoppages reportedly occurred over "procedural matters . . . to hurry along the dispute settlement process."[16] The state's director of conciliation and arbitration related that there

are some who say that "well there were very few [strikes] prior [to the law]." While that may be true, we cannot forget that in [the two prior years] intense feelings began to develop throughout the state over negotiations which became very lengthy without producing voluntary agreements, and there was no place for these disputes to go.[17]

The question raised here is a fairly direct one. Do statutory impasse procedures reduce strikes? The answer is less direct: the evidence is mixed but the amount of activity is small enough that the answer does not much matter (except to those directly affected).

Many have suggested that the best way to ensure motivation of the parties to bargain is to allow them to strike over impasses. Economics professor Charles W. Baird takes a contrary view, expressing a dim view of the effectiveness of strike authorizing legislation.

The claim . . . that legalizing public sector strikes will actually decrease the incidence of strikes is counterfactual. Pennsylvania legalized public sector strikes in 1970 whereupon there followed a thirteen-fold increase in such strikes . . . Nationally, the average number of public sector strikes per state, per year was 1.34 before the adoption of collective bargaining legislation and 5.00 after the adoption of collective bargaining legislation. . . . The increased incidence of strikes was not due merely to a secular increase in the propensity of government employees to strike. Except in 1961 the average number of strikes per state among employees not covered by collective bargaining legislation . . . was substantially less than among employees that were covered by such legislation.[18]

Negotiating in Future Years

Becoming an informed negotiator is the key to avoiding impasse. The practitioner needs to be informed on issues and the administration of bargaining and impasse resolution. Authors at the University of South Carolina and Purdue University have simulated bargaining with "naive negotiators." The more training the bargainers received, the closer the parties were to reaching a settlement.[19] This book has already moved the practitioner out of the category of "naive negotiator." Further experience and attention to the principles presented should reduce undesirable impasses, increase the likelihood that impasses can be resolved, and help maintain the bargaining relationship in the event the impasse goes to arbitration.

IMPASSE PROCEDURES AND ARBITRATION OUTCOMES

The question was raised earlier concerning the resort to impasse resolution procedures and the outcome resulting. It has been established that impasses are more likely to occur when there are statuatory impasse procedures. But what effect does having these procedures have on the salaries that result from their use? Can unions/agencies do better in arbitration than in negotiations? The general answer to the first question is that the availability of impasse procedures tends to cause negotiated salaries to be a little bit higher than they would otherwise be. While overall public sector legislation cannot be labeled pro-labor or pro-management, the advent of impasse resolution procedures is generally seen to have been pro-labor. Once the procedures are available, however, there is no discernable difference between salaries that are negotiated and salaries awarded by a neutral.[20]

This point is made so that parties who have been introduced to public sector impasse procedures through this book will never succumb to the temptation to prefer the services of a neutral to the advantages of a negotiated settlement. The authors view the neutral as a physician called in to treat one symptom of an ailing labor relationship. The services of the physician should not be performed to good health. The neutral should be called upon only when the labor relationship requires professional assistance.

EVOLUTION OF
LABOR/MANAGEMENT COOPERATION

Many labor relations observers have found that times of moderate, but not extreme, financial stress are most likely to produce increased labor–management cooperation. Professor Sanford Jacoby concludes that "unions and employers will voluntarily work together to improve productivity only within an intermediate range of economic stress."[21] The Scanlon Plans of the post–World War II era similarly saw cooperation as most likely only when the parties saw cooperation as necessary to maintain a competitive (hence operating and employing) position in the market.

The public sector has experienced moderate financial stress in recent years. Many agency budgets have not kept pace with inflation or workloads. These stresses have generally not been severe; rarely is the survivability of an agency threatened. But stresses have made it difficult for agencies to provide employees with anticipated improvements in salaries and benefits. One possible, and often actual, consequence of these stresses is conflict rather than cooperation. The press has discussed the increasing conflict observed in some towns and school districts as a natural outgrowth of financial pressures. The authors feel that the public sector need not be different from the private sector, that increased financial pressures could be the catalyst for greater cooperation.

The pressing question for agencies and unions, then, is how can a relationship become more cooperative when financial pressures are increasing? Cooperation centers on negotiations. Good negotiations require good information and understanding of the process. One concrete way for negotiators to show an attitude of cooperation is to give the parties who sit across the bargaining table a useful gift. The authors highly recommend copies of a book subtitled "Negotiating Agreement Without Giving In." The formal title of this informal book is *Getting to YES*. It is designed for a general audience, inexpensive (under $10 in paperback), and easy reading. Before giving it away, though, the negotiating team should read it.

With a subtitle that includes "without giving in," the gift is sure to be seen as a cooperative move. But the book is not about winning; it is about getting the bargaining process to succeed by focusing on issues. The following anecdote from the book's concluding remarks makes that point.

In 1964 an American father and his twelve-year-old son were enjoying a beautiful Sunday in Hyde Park, London, playing catch with a Frisbee. Few in England had seen a Frisbee at that time and a small group of strollers gathered to watch this strange sport. Finally, one Homburg-clad Britisher came over to the father: "Sorry to bother you. Been watching you a quarter of an hour. Who's *winning*?[22]

Both parties can win when negotiators look for ways to meet both parties' concerns rather than their demands.

At the State Level—A Structural Initiative

Massachusetts, in response to an aggressive political climate, adopted a novel approach to resolve management's dissatisfaction with mandatory interest arbitration and labor's demand for closure in bargaining. The firefighters' union represented its constituents and most police associations in negotiating an agreement with the Massachusetts League of Cities and Towns. The state legislature effectively ratified this agreement by passing a statute virtually identical in its terms.[23] This agreement established the bipartisan Joint Labor–Management Committee (JLMC): six management representatives, six labor representatives, and two neutrals (one of whom chaired the committee). The brainchild of Professor Dunlop, formerly secretary of labor, the JLMC

was empowered to take jurisdiction in any dispute over a police or fire fighter contract, whether or not they were petitioned by the parties for such jurisdiction. Through a variety of informal mechanisms as well as formal procedures, the Committee was to seek to mediate as much as possible and was given the power to arbitrate in those instances in which a mediated solution was not possible.[24]

Professor Dunlop notes that the JLMC "was created . . . is manned [and] . . . is operated by the parties" themselves.[25] Though the JLMC was initiated in response to strong adversarial political actions previously undertaken by the parties, it is a singular example of state level labor–management cooperation.[26]

CONCLUSION

On the one hand, statutory impasse resolution procedures offer parties additional assistance in resolving difficulties that arise in the attempt to come to a collective bargaining agreement. On the other hand, statutory procedures that involve a closure step, such as arbitration, offer a party the opportunity to substitute a neutral's decision for a negotiated settlement. This chapter summarized the results of modeling experiments and empirical research; five major conclusions were reached.

When practitioners bargain with a good faith attitude, mediation is likely to be a very useful tool to break an impasse. The converse is also true; mediation is rarely successful at resolving an impasse when one or both of the parties are not bargaining in good faith.

Fact finding is most likely to be successful when there are honest disagreements or when one party faces political pressures to hold to a hard line.

Parties who have resorted to statutory procedures in the past are more likely to repeat this behavior. This narcotic effect wears off after some time as parties discover that adjudicated settlements are inferior to negotiated settlements.

Increasing the number of impasse resolution steps increases their use. No single set of procedures seems to be significantly more successful than others. It appears appropriate for jurisdictions to continue refining their procedures to match local needs.

Investigations into strike (or other job actions) show no steady pattern related to the impasse resolution structure. This is disquieting to some since strike avoidance is one of the reasons most commonly given as a reason for collective bargaining statutes.

Nonetheless, public sector strikes remain rare by most measures. Practitioners are warned that the absence of a strike is hardly proof of good labor–management relations.

Considerable time has been spent to discover if arbitration awards differ systematically from negotiated agreements. Time and time again the answer is no. Parties need to work together to shape an agreement that most closely meets their needs and individual situations. While arbitrators may fashion a package that has the same overall dollar value, the distribution of dollars may not be quite what the parties would have chosen for themselves had they been able to break the deadlock in negotiations. Arbitration remains a viable method of bringing closure to a dispute. But it is still a second-best solution.

Many avenues remain open for increased labor–management cooperation. Agencies and unions can work together to become better negotiators. This will decrease the likelihood of impasse, particularly impasses unresolved by mediation or fact finding. Increased cooperation often takes the path of structural changes in the handling of disputes. Some jurisdictions allow parties a great deal of latitude in fashioning their own dispute resolution techniques should they be so inclined. The options are plentiful. Examining those options together furthers the attitude of cooperation that must have positive consequences for the bargaining relationship.

NOTES

1. Thomas A. Kochan, Mordecai Mironi, Ronald G. Ehrenberg, Jean Baderschneider, and Todd Jick, *Dispute Resolution under Fact-finding and Arbitration: An Empirical Analysis* (New York: American Arbitration Association, 1979), 54 (hereafter cited as Kochan, 1979).

2. Kochan, 1979, 53.

3. Kochan, 1979, 54.

4. Thomas A. Kochan and Jean Baderschneider, "Dependence on Impasse Procedures: Police and Firefighters in New York State," *Industrial and Labor Relations Review* 31, no. 4 (July 1978): 434.

5. *Final Report of the Governor's Committee on Public Employee Relations* (Albany: State of New York, 1966), 33; as reported in Kochan, 1979, 6.

6. Kochan, 1979, 25–26.

7. Compare a later review of the New York study and the response of the original researchers. Richard J. Butler and Ronald G. Ehrenberg's "Estimating the Narcotic Effect of Public Sector Impasse Procedures," *Industrial and Labor Relations Review* 35, no. 1 (October 1981): 3–20, and Thomas A. Kochan and Jean Baderschneider's "Estimating the Narcotic Effect: Choosing Techniques that Fit the Problem," *Industrial and Labor Relations Review* 35, no. 1 (October 1981): 21–28. A follow-up study supported the assertion that the narcotic effect was of short or intermediate duration. James A. Chelius and Marion M. Extejt, "The Narcotic Effect of Impasse-Resolution Procedures," *Industrial and Labor Relations Review* 38, no. 4 (July 1985): 629–630.

8. The New York law previously allowed referral of impasse issues to the legislature for determination if fact finding was unsuccessful at the dispute.

9. This happened in Massachusetts when that state added arbitration as a final step for firefighters and police. But one author noted that the increase was temporary and offered the possibility that parties might try arbitration just to find out how well it worked. Jonathan Brock, *Bargaining Beyond Impasse: Joint Resolution of Public Sector Labor Disputes* (Boston: Auburn House, 1982), 38 (hereafter cited as Brock, 1982).

10. Kochan, 1979, 37, 158.

11. Kochan, 1979, 158.

12. Kochan, 1979, 92.

13. Daniel G. Gallagher and Richard Pegnetter, "Impasse Resolution Under the Iowa Multistep Procedure," *Industrial and Labor Relations Review* 32, no. 3 (April 1979): 327–338.

14. William J. Walsh, "An Institutional and Economic Analysis of the Teacher Collective Bargaining Act," Ph.D. dissertation, Indiana University, 1986, 220.

15. William M. Weinberg, "A Comment on the Legislative History," *Interest Arbitration: Proceedings of an IMLR Conference* (Brunswick, N.J.: Institute of Management and Labor Relations, Rutgers—The State University of New Jersey, 1980), 5.

16. Ibid., 7.

17. James W. Mastriani, "Compulsory Interest Arbitration: An Analysis of the First Two Years' Experience," *Interest Arbitration: Proceedings of an IMLR Conference* (Brunswick, N.J.: Institute of Management and Labor Relations, Rutgers—The State University of New Jersey, 1980), 11–12.

18. Charles W. Baird, "Strikes Against Government: The California Supreme Court Decision," *Government Union Review* 7, no. 1 (Winter 1986): 22–23.

19. Angelo S. DeNisi and James B. Dwarkin, "Final Offer Arbitration and the Naive Negotiator," *Industrial and Labor Relations Review* 35, no. 1 (October 1981): 78–87.

20. Peter Feuille and John Thomas Delaney, "Collective Bargaining, Interest Arbitration, and Police Salaries," *Industrial and Labor Relations Review* 39, no. 2 (January 1986): 228–240; Brock, 1982, 38, indicates that this is the substance of the Sloane Report for the particular case of Massachusetts.

21. Sanford M. Jacoby, "Union–Management Cooperation in the United States: Lessons from the 1920s," *Industrial and Labor Relations Review* 37, no. 1 (October 1983): 18.

22. Roger Fisher and William Ury, *Getting to YES: Negotiating Agreement Without Giving In* (New York: Penguin, 1981), 154.

23. Brock, 1982, 25–26.

24. Brock, 1982, 44, 47.

25. Brock, 1982, v.

26. Brock, 1982, presents a guide for establishing such a joint committee for those practitioners who operate at the statewide level within their own organizations.

9

Bargaining During the Life of the Contract

Consistent with the requirements of the Taft-Hartley Act, parties are required to continue to bargain in good faith after the contract has been negotiated and implemented. The nature of the issues and the bargaining required changes once the contract has been implemented. This chapter examines the legal requirements imposed on parties once they have the contract.

This chapter also examines the law concerning the modification or termination of a contract that is in force, the parties' obligations to meet and confer over issues that arise during the life of the contract, and the law concerning grievances and their arbitration.

TERMINATION OR MODIFICATION OF A CONTRACT

The dynamics of the U.S. economy and the uncertainty under which most parties to collective bargaining operate cause demands for mid-contract modifications or even contract terminations. Changes in agreed-to contract provisions are not specifically prohibited by law. Changes in an existing contract, however, are subject to the same types of requirements that exist for the original negotiation of the agreement. The parties must meet and confer in good faith and negotiate concerning proposed changes in the agreement or termination of the contract.

The duty to bargain once a contract is negotiated extends unaltered from the obligation to bargain in good faith in negotiating the contract. The NLRB has prohibited employer unilateral actions over mandatory issues of collective bargaining.[1] In general, this same obligation exists in the public sector, except where the collective bargaining law or other applicable statutes modify this rule of law.[2] Legislative action can modify a negotiated agreement in the public sector, the same as it can in the private sector. In New York, the governor signed legislation prohibiting the negotiation of pensions after several contracts were negotiated specifying pension rights. The American Federation of State County and Municipal Employees appealed to the New York PERB claiming that the governor engaged in a prohibited practice.[3] The PERB drew a distinction between the governor's function as chief administrative officer of the state of New York and his legislative function. If the governor had changed the treatment of pensions under the contract as chief executive officer, then he would have committed a prohibited practice. In this case a bill was passed by the legislature and forwarded to the governor for his signature. The governor signed the bill into law rather than vetoing it. His action was legislative and therefore within his authority under the New York Constitution and cannot be construed as a prohibited practice.

A majority of state collective bargaining laws make no reference to the modification or termination of an existing agreement. The Oregon statute requires that certain terms and conditions of employment may not be changed during arbitration.[4] This type of requirement is not unusual, however, the types of notification requirements found in the Taft-Hartley Act are unusual. The Taft-Hartley Act requires 90 days notification to the other party and the Federal Mediation and Conciliation Service of a modification of a contract. Because most public sector contracts are for one year, such notice requirements would have almost no effect.[5]

ISSUES THAT ARISE DURING LIFE OF CONTRACT

There are several ways for issues to arise during the life of the contract. Grievances over the interpretation and application of the agreement require bargaining during the life of the contract. These issues are discussed in the following section of this chapter. The parties are sometimes faced with issues that were not contemplated during contract negotiations. In addition to one party or the other requesting modification or termination, legislative action or financial problems can cause the need to add to, subtract from, or change an existing contract. The most common example of this situation is where state aid to education or municipalities is reduced legislatively. Iowa during the mid-1980s suffered significant reductions in state aid to education due to the farm crisis, causing the renegotiation of several collective bargaining agreements.

In general, the obligation to bargain in good faith extends to legislative changes during the life of a contract that impacts a collective bargaining agreement.[6]

ARBITRATION AND GRIEVANCES

Collective bargaining statutes frequently specifically authorize the arbitration of grievances. For example, the Minnesota Public Employment Relations Act states in pertinent part:

Section 179.70 Contracts; Grievances; Arbitration.—Subdivision 1. A written contract or memorandum of contract containing the agreed upon terms and conditions of employment and such other matters as may be agreed upon by the employer and exclusive representative shall be executed by the parties . . . All contracts shall include a grievance procedure which shall provide compulsory binding arbitration of grievances including all disciplinary actions.[7]

Several other states specifically authorize and/or require the final and binding arbitration of grievances within the expressed language of the collective bargaining statute, such as Washington,[8] Pennsylvania,[9] and Kansas.[10]

Statutory authority for final and binding arbitration of grievances essentially brings private sector law concerning the enforcement and finality of arbitration awards to the public sector.[11] Problems arise when there is no specific authorization of the arbitration of grievances contained in the collective bargaining statute. Each of these bodies of law is reviewed in the following sections.

Statutory Authorization and Private Sector Law

The courts have consistently ruled that where a collective bargaining statute either requires or authorizes the final and binding arbitration of grievances that private sector law provides guidance.[12] Private sector law is therefore applicable in these jurisdictions.

Until 1957, whether collective bargaining contracts in general and arbitration agreements in particular were legally enforceable depended upon the state court having jurisdiction over the matter. Most state courts refused to enforce due to doubt as to the legal standing of unions to enter into contracts binding the employees they represented.[13] The Taft-Hartley Act specifically authorized suits for violations of collective bargaining agreements.[14] Section 301 of the Taft-Hartley Act appeared to make collective bargaining agreements and arbitration clauses enforceable through the federal court system. Final determination, however, had to await Supreme Court action. The court settled the issue with its decision in *Textile Workers Union of America v. Lincoln Mills of Alabama* in June 1957.[15] In this case, the parties had executed a collective bargaining agreement containing an arbitration clause. The employer refused to submit to arbitration, and the union brought suit under Section 301 of the Taft-Hartley Act to compel arbitration. The Supreme Court voted to enforce the agreement to arbitrate, and in so doing established the Taft-Hartley Act as statutory authority for court enforcement of labor agreements.

Arbitration's role in labor relations was solidified and its relationship to the courts defined by three Supreme Court decisions rendered on June 20, 1960, landmark decisions commonly referred to as the Steelworkers Trilogy. In the first two cases, the *United Steelworkers v. Warrior and Gulf Navigation Company*[16] and *United Steelworkers v. American Manufacturing Company*,[17] the Supreme Court took the position that, unless excluded from grievance arbitration by clear and specific contract language, all issues are arbitrable, not just those a court may deem meritorious. Stated differently, arbitrability is a matter for the arbitrator to decide, not the courts. In the third case, *United Steelworkers v. Enterprise Wheel & Car Corp.*, the court held that the courts cannot overrule an arbitrator's decision simply because they disagree with the arbitrator's construction and interpretation of the contract.[18] The court reasoned that it was the arbitrator's opinion that was bargained for, not that of the courts. The courts, therefore, exceed their authority whenever they substitute their judgment for that of the arbitrator. In short, the Supreme Court's decisions in the trilogy cases established arbitration as a legitimate method of dispute resolution not inferior to judicial processes.

Fair Representation

The courts can review an arbitrator's award where the arbitrator has failed to conduct a fair and proper hearing,[19] the arbitrator has clearly exceeded his or her authority under the labor agreement,[20] the grievance involves violations of constitutional or statutory rights as well as contract rights,[21] or the union has not discharged its obligation to represent fairly an employee. The latter is particularly relevant to the present discussion.

The Taft-Hartley Act, Civil Service Reform Act, and state statutes that provide for exclusive employee representation by labor unions for purposes of collective bargaining also require fair representation by those same unions. The right of exclusive representation carries with it the responsibility to represent fairly members of the bargaining unit—a quid pro quo relationship.

The duty to represent fairly involves both substantive and procedural requirements. It requires unions, when representing employees during contract administration, to conduct full and competent investigations of all matters reasonably pertaining to the grievance and to process grievances in good faith without caprice, malice, and without an intent to discriminate with regard to grievants' race, gender, age, place of national origin, religion, or union membership status.[22] Failure to meet any of these obligations may subject the union to a charge of failure to represent fairly and, ultimately, make them liable for back pay.

In *Hines v. Anchor Motor Freight*, several employees were discharged for allegedly defrauding their employer.[23] Although the union processed their grievances through the grievance procedure to arbitration, it did not conduct an adequate investigation nor did it provide a competent defense in the case. The arbitrator sustained the discharges, and the employees sued the union for failure to represent fairly and to vacate the arbitrator's award. After the arbitrator issued the award in this matter, additional evidence was uncovered that demonstrated that the employees were unjustly discharged. The lower federal courts refused upon the basis of the additional evidence to displace the arbitrator's award citing the *Steelworkers Trilogy*. The Supreme Court, however, reversed the lower courts and vacated the arbitration award. The employees were reinstated and damages were apportioned (back pay and legal fees) between the employer and the union—the equal sharing of liability was justified on the grounds that it was the employer who wrongly discharged the employees, but the union failed to secure prompt reinstatement through fair representation.

Good faith and nondiscriminatory grievance representation, however, are not sufficient to protect a union from a charge of failure to represent fairly. The union must also follow proper procedure, as established by the U.S. Supreme Court in *Bowen v. U.S. Postal Service*.[24] The case involved a wrongfully discharged employee who brought suit in federal court against the Postal Service for discharge without just cause, and his union, the American Postal Workers Union, for arbitrary and capricious handling of the grievance and breaching its duty to represent fairly. They had found the grievance to be without merit and decided accordingly not to process it to arbitration. Reversing an appellate court ruling for the union, the Supreme Court concurred with the federal district court that the union had not fairly represented the employee. Interestingly, the court found that the union had honestly addressed the grievance and had not behaved in a capricious or discriminatory manner. The court also found that the union had conducted a proper investigation. The union fell short, according to the court, because it failed to provide an explanation to the aggrieved employee for not proceeding to arbitration. The court reasoned that, had the union done so, the aggrieved employee could have countered the errors the union had, in good faith, made in determining that the grievance had no merit. The court upheld the federal district court's apportionment of damages (back pay) between the employer and the union. The employer was deemed liable for back pay from the time of unlawful discharge until the time when an arbitrator would have reinstated the employee had the union properly represented him, with the union liable for the remainder.

Another procedural requirement for an employee to bring a successful suit against his or her union for failure to represent fairly concerns time limits. In *DelCostello v. IBT 113*, the U.S. Supreme Court adopted a six-month time limit for the initiation of such suits.[25] By doing so, the court provided unions some measure of protection from large back pay and damage awards; the employee cannot lay back and wait several years before filing in the hope of achieving what amounts to a paid vacation. In short, to be successful, suits for breach of fair representation must be filed in a timely manner—within six months of the breach.

The rules of law established in private sector litigation have been consistently applied by state courts and administrative law agencies under collective bargaining statutes requiring or authorizing final and binding arbitration. In this arena again, the state experience has been to adopt an approach that has been pioneered and found serviceable in the private sector.

There is another aspect to statutory authorization of arbitration found in the public sector that does not exist in the private sector. Several statutes, including those in Minnesota and Massachusetts, require arbitrators to adhere to the professional ethics promulgated by the National Academy of Arbitrators, Federal Mediation and Conciliation Service, and the American Arbitration Association. This code of professional responsibility requires neutrality, confidentiality, and prompt issuance of awards, and governs the arbitrators' relations with the parties and administrative agencies, among other standards. The legislative intent is to assure a high standard of neutral conduct in resolving grievances between public agencies and their unions.[26]

In these jurisdictions arbitration is as firmly established as it is in the private sector. The enforcement of contracts through grievance/arbitration mechanisms assures that negotiated contracts are meaningful and binding upon the respective parties. In the absence of arbitration, employers risk only lawsuits. The cost and time involved in suits for enforcement of contracts reduce the probability that litigation will occur. However, if litigation does occur, the potential liability generally increases substantially. For example, if an employee is wrongfully discharged under a contract with an arbitration clause, the remedy applied by an arbitrator will be back pay if the grievance is meritorious. In the absence of arbitration, the full range of remedies applied by the courts, including exemplary damages, pain and suffering, legal fees, and real damages, could be applied to meritorious complaints. In other words, there is a trade-off: less likely litigation for potentially much higher damage awards.

In the Absence of Statutory Authorization

The state courts have not treated the arbitration of grievances as liberally in the absence of statutory requirements or authorization for the process. In *Wichita Public Schools Employees Union, Local 513 v. Smith*, the Kansas Court stated that the Kansas arbitration act

must be construed to apply only to private industry, at least until such time as the legislature shows a definite intent to include political subdivisions.[27]

The reasoning in the *Wichita* case represents a majority view of the judiciary in jurisdictions without specific statutory authorization or requirements to arbitrate grievances. Courts have consistently found that if there are limitations on school boards or city commissions delegating authority, then the arbitration of grievances is an illegal delegation of authority.[28] If delegation of authority is not limited, or exceptions to proscriptions of delegation of authority are found in the collective bargaining (or other) statutes, then the enforceability of arbitration awards becomes less certain.

In jurisdictions where there is no clear authorization of arbitration and delegation of authority is not proscribed, there is a large area of uncertainty. Several jurisdictions permit the de facto arbitration of grievances in such a legal environment. There is, however, one further avenue of attack on arbitration in this arena. The courts have found that legislators are responsible for making public policy. If a public sector labor contract is to be enforced in the courts, then the public policy making authority of the legislature is being illegally usurped and is therefore not permissible.[29]

Meet and confer states have had arbitration of grievance matters authorized by statute. For example, in Indiana, state employees were permitted to seek resolution of disputes concerning their terms and conditions of employment established by law to be resolved by an arbitrator. Such arrangements are relatively rare and are subject to substantial interference from the courts.[30]

In several states there are substitutes for arbitration that do not involve court litigation. States such as Kansas, Iowa, and Indiana provide "due process" machinery for disciplinary matters and contract renewals for public school teachers. Civil service boards and other similar decision-making authorities exist in several states to provide an informal process to resolve disputes between employees (or their representatives) and the public employer.[31] The experience of this substitute procedure varies widely across jurisdictions, and very few generalizations can be offered.

SUMMARY AND CONCLUSIONS

The obligation to bargain in good faith extends to the administration of a collective bargaining agreement. Termination and modification of collective bargaining agreements are rarely addressed by statutes because most jurisdictions negotiate one-year agreements. There are financial and other reasons that parties may be required to reopen collective bargaining agreements during their effective life. Iowa, in particular, during the farm crisis years, experienced delayed negotiations and reopened contracts because of state financial shortfalls.

The arbitration of grievances is often authorized or required by state collective bargaining statutes. In jurisdictions where grievance procedures and arbitration are either authorized or required, the state courts have typically followed the rules of law arising out of the interpretation and application of the Taft-Hartley Act. Arbitration awards are fully enforceable in the courts and are not generally subject to review by the judiciary. Exceptions to this rule exist. If an arbitrator exceeds his or her authority or engages in misconduct, or if the union breaches its duty to represent fairly, an arbitration award may be reviewed and set aside by the courts.

In jurisdictions without enabling legislation for grievance arbitration, there is less acceptance of the process. The courts have found that public employers cannot delegate authority to arbitrators if legislatively or constitutionally barred from doing so. In such cases arbitration of labor disputes cannot be enforced through the courts. Courts have also sometimes found that arbitration encroaches on the public policy making authority of the legislative branch of government, and therefore awards cannot be enforced in the courts.

NOTES

1. *NLRB v. Katz*, 369 U.S. 736 (1962).
2. *Town of Stratford*, Connecticut State Board of Labor Relations, Decision No. 1069 (1972).
3. *State of New York v. AFSCME Council 82* New York PERB Case No. U-0984 (1974).
4. Chapter 243, Title 22 Oregon Revised Statutes, Section 243.756.
5. Section 8(d).
6. *Ligonier Valley School District* Case No. PERA-C-1542-W, Pennsylvania Labor Relations Board (1972).
7. Sections 179.61 through 179.76 Minnesota Statutes.
8. Section 41.56.122 (2)Revised Code of Washington, specifically requires binding arbitration of labor disputes.
9. Sections 5 through 8 Public Law 237, No. 111, Pennsylvania requires arbitration of disputes for police and firefighters.
10. Section 72–5424, Kansas Statutes Annotated authorizes parties to enter into agreements to arbitrate grievances in public education. Few school districts, however, have negotiated grievance procedures ending in final and binding arbitration. In 1990 only five school districts had final and binding arbitration, and two others permit "advisory" arbitration of grievances.
11. *Providence Teachers Union Local 958 v. School Committee of Providence*, 108 R.I. 444, 276 A.2d 762 (1971) is the principle case cited as authority in such matters.
12. Ibid.
13. Clarence R. Deitsch and David A. Dilts, *The Arbitration of Rights Disputes in the Public Sector* (Westport, Conn.: Quorum Books, 1990), 40–41.
14. Section 301.
15. 77 S.Ct. 913 (1957).
16. 363 U.S. 574 (1960).
17. 363 U.S. 564 (1960).
18. 363 U.S. 593 (1960).

19. *Spielberg Manufacturing Company*, 112 NLRB 1080 (1955).

20. *Torrington v. Metal Product Workers Local 645*, 363 F.2d 677 (1966).

21. *Alexander v. Gardner-Lenver Co.*, 415 U.S. 36 (1974).

22. *Vaca v. Sipes*, 363 U.S. 171 (1967).

23. 424 U.S. 554 (1976).

24. 459 U.S. 212 (1983).

25. 462 U.S. 151 (1983).

26. See Deitsch and Dilts, Chapter 8 and Appendix 2.

27. 397 P.2d 357 (1964).

28. For example, see *Rockland Professional Fire Fighters Association v. City of Rockland.* (Maine) 261 A.2d 418 (1970).

29. *Fellows v. La Tronica*, 151 Colo. 300 (1962).

30. David A. Dilts and Clarence R. Deitsch, "*Rockville Training Center v. Alvin Peschke:* Vindication of Court Rationale Underlying the Steelworkers Trilogy," *Employee Relations Law Journal* 10, no. 1 (1984): 95–105.

31. Indiana State Personnel Act (I.C. 1971, 4-15-2-1, 4-15-2-46). Indiana Statutes Annotated.

10

Public Sector Labor Law: Conclusions, Trends, and Possibilities

Labor law in the private sector dates from the late 1920s, with the passage of Railway Labor Act in 1926. The first public sector collective bargaining law passed by a state legislature was thirty-six years later. Even considering the federal sector, collective bargaining was late in coming to the public sector. Even so, because unions were predominately a private sector phenomenon, unions in the public sector have not yet been extensively examined.

Add to these complications the fact that there are nearly three dozen states that have independently passed public sector labor laws. There is virtually nothing written that focuses exclusively on labor law in state and local government. The purpose of this book was to present a generally applicable examination of labor law in state and local governments.

It was not the purpose of the authors to do a scientific examination of the labor law and draw firm inference from the evidence gathered for this book. There are, however, several conclusions that can be drawn concerning the collective bargaining statutes presently in evidence governing labor relations for state and local governments. The first section of this chapter presents the conclusions that can be tentatively drawn from the research required to write this book. Brief discussions concerning observed trends in the law and possibilities for labor law at the state and local levels are offered next.

LABOR LAW: THE EVIDENCE

Labor law at the state and local government level has been criticized as being a patchwork of confused and unrelated approaches to governing labor–management relations. Undoubtedly it appears that state and local governments have made law from whole cloth to suit the biases, needs, and/or perceptions of policymakers. In fact, there is significant diversity among jurisdictions in the laws that have been enacted. What is surprising is that there is also a great deal of consistency in how several types of problems are handled by jurisdictions. Some interesting conclusions can be drawn.

Present Status of Law

There are only eleven states that do not protect collective bargaining rights for at least some segment of the public sector work force. Over half of those states that protect public employee collective bargaining rights have omnibus bargaining statutes. The states with collective bargaining bills are the wealthiest, most-heavily industrialized (hence unionized) states in the union.

The states with no public sector labor relations laws are typically southern or sparsely populated western states without significant industrial bases. Virtually every one of the states without a public sector collective bargaining law has a right-to-work law.

The evidence suggests that there is a strong correlation between a lack of public sector collective bargaining rights and other anti-union legislation. The political environment within these states is clearly different from the remainder of the states with respect to union issues. Little more inference can be drawn from this limited information.

Comparability of Statutes

It is surprising that there are several consistencies in the labor laws observed. The majority of the state collective bargaining statutes were enacted in the 1970s. Few were enacted in the 1960s, and even fewer were enacted in the 1980s. The only major omnibus collective bargaining law initially passed in the 1980s was in Ohio.

There are several provisions of the various statutes that are very similar. Most states had very similar unfair or prohibited practice provisions. The majority of states made provisions in their statutes for the conduct of certification elections and for the investigation and adjudication of unfair labor practices. These provisions of state collective bargaining laws were, for the most part, similar to the provisions found in the Taft-Hartley Act. It was common for provisions to be added that concerned issues unique to state and local agency needs, such as good faith participation in impasse procedures. There were also a few states, such as Montana, whose laws differed somewhat in these matters.

The impasse procedures adopted by most states were also very similar. Most states had multiple-step impasse procedures that began with mediation and ended with final and binding arbitration of interest disputes (twenty-two such states). Every state that protected strike activity also had final and binding arbitration provisions in the collective bargaining statute. Another eleven states had only two-step impasse procedures—mediation and fact finding. When fact finding was specified as the final step in impasse procedures, there were generally no other mechanisms offered for closure to negotiations. Again, the majority of states without final and binding arbitration that had collective bargaining laws were southern or sparsely populated western states. In this category were also a few relatively small northeastern states.

Employee rights were specifically identified in virtually all the collective bargaining statutes, but less than half of the collective bargaining statutes listed employer rights. The employee rights listed in collective bargaining laws were also very similar to the Section 7 rights found in the Taft-Hartley Act.

The language found in state collective bargaining laws concerning the parties' obligations to bargain in good faith was also very similar to the provisions of Section 8 (d) of Taft-Hartley. With the exception of the time frames specified in Section 8 (d) of the National Labor Relations Act, the requirements to meet and confer at reasonable times and places were contained in all but two of the collective bargaining laws examined. A slim majority of state statutes specified that collective bargaining agreements must be one-year contracts, or if they are two-year contracts, they must contain reopeners that coincided with the state financing calendar. This explains why the time frames for modification and termination of the agreements were not included in state collective bargaining statutes.

Virtually all of the state collective bargaining laws also created an administrative law agency charged with similar responsibilities as those specified for the National Labor Relations Board. Virtually none of the meet and confer laws created an administrative law agency for enforcement of the act.

The court and administrative law cases that are of landmark significance or potential seem to have been heard primarily in the mid-1970s. The constitutional matters concerning the validity of the legislation and employee rights were predominately in the late 1960s and early 1970s. However, there seems to have been a trend in that most of the litigation occurs within the first three to five years of the passage of the collective bargaining bill. It appears that parties try to set the boundaries of the interpretation and application of the statutory language at an early stage so that they can get on with the business of day-to-day labor relations. This result is consistent with earlier reported research.[1]

In short, there are many general trends with some individual variations among the 36 states that have collective bargaining laws. Most of these states seem to have adopted provisions that closely mirror those found in the Taft-Hartley Act with some fine tuning for the level of government and local conditions.

TRENDS

There appears to be little evidence to suggest that there will be many states adopting new collective bargaining statutes. Ohio enacted a comprehensive an omnibus collective bargaining law in 1983. Since then, only Indiana is active in this arena. In 1990 the governor of Indiana issued an executive order permitting the recognition and negotiations with unions representing employees of state agencies. The overwhelming majority of state employees voted for union representation, and there has been very little movement towards the passage of an omnibus collective bargaining bill promised by the governor.

The bills introduced during 1991 in the Indiana legislature excluded several significant classes of public employees, most notably employees of institutions of higher education. Whether Indiana will have a collective bargaining bill for state employees that extends to local governmental employees is doubtful due to the legislature not having a majority in support of such a bill. It must be remembered that Indiana is the only industrialized state in the Great Lakes region that ever had a right-to-work law and has never been among the leaders in protective legislation for unions or the working class.

There is little or no hope of reviving the federal level legislation once proposed to grant collective bargaining to state and local government employees in the United States. The conservative swing experienced in the 1980s probably makes it impossible that such legislation will even be introduced in the near future.

POSSIBILITIES

From the trends it is obvious that there is still potential for states to enact and amend their present statutes to make for greater consistency in the treatment of public employees across state boundaries. One realistic possibility and recommendation is the formulation and adoption of uniform state collective bargaining bills. James McClimon (once director of the Iowa PERB and now a member of that board) and others were heavily consulted as Indiana considered the passage of a collective bargaining bill.

Given that the Uniform Arbitration Act has been adopted in a large majority of states, it would appear reasonable and beneficial that there be some uniformity introduced to state collective bargaining bills. An approach similar to that taken in formulating and enacting the Uniform Arbitration Act would provide for shared experience of administrative law agencies and establish a body of court precedents that would be less confusing. Further, consistency in the treatment of public employees across state boundaries may prove beneficial in reducing turnover and lending some predictability to employment and conditions across jurisdictions. Further, consistency across jurisdictions would make the education of public personnel and labor relations practitioners far easier; hence it could be reasonably inferred that better trained and more-experienced personnel and labor relations experts would become more readily available to public agencies and unions.

AFTERWORD

The paucity of research on public sector labor law was painfully evident in doing the research for this book. There is a disparate need for more legal research on state collective bargaining statutes. There are a wide array of state-specific law review articles and some attempts at comparisons or broader research, but legal scholars have scarcely scratched the surface of this body of law.

The authors hope that this modest first attempt at a unified approach to the examination of state collective bargaining and meet and confer statutes will help both scholars and practitioners.

NOTE

1. Stanley W. Elsea and David A. Dilts, "Unfair Labor Practice Charges Under State Bargaining Laws: Indiana, Iowa, and Kansas," *Labor Law Journal* 41, no. 6 (June 1990): 376–380.

Appendix

Public Employment Relations Board Rules and Regulations of the Iowa Code

PUBLIC EMPLOYMENT RELATIONS BOARD[621]

[Prior to 11/5/86, Public Employment Relations Board (660)]

CHAPTER 1
GENERAL PROVISIONS
1.1(20) Construction and severability
1.2(20) General agency description
1.3(20) General course and method of operation
1.4(20) Method of obtaining information and making submissions or requests
1.5(20) Petition for adoption of rules
1.6(20) Definitions
1.7(20) Computation of time

CHAPTER 2
GENERAL PRACTICE AND HEARING PROCEDURES
2.1(20) Hearing—time and place— administrative law judge
2.2(20) Notice of hearing—contents
2.3(20) Failure to appear
.4(20) Intervention and additional parties
2.5(20) Continuance
2.6(20) Appearances and conduct of parties
2.7(20) Evidence—objections
2.8(20) Order of procedure
2.9(20) Amendments
2.10(20) Briefs and arguments
2.11(20) Sequestration of witnesses
2.12(20) Subpoenas
2.13(20) Form of documents
2.14(20) Captions
2.15(20) Service of pleadings and other papers
2.16(20) Consolidation
2.17(20) Prohibition against testimony of mediators, fact-finders, arbitrators and board employees
2.18(20) Delivery of decisions and orders
2.19(20) Stays of agency action
2.20(20) Ex parte communications
2.21(20) Transcripts of record
2.22(20) Dismissal

CHAPTER 3
PROHIBITED PRACTICE COMPLAINTS
3.1(20) Filing of complaint
3.2(20) Contents of complaint

3.3(20) Clarification of complaint
3.4(20) Service of complaint
3.5(20) Answer to complaint
3.6(20) Withdrawal of complaint
3.7(20) Amendment of complaint or answer
3.8(20) Investigation of complaint
3.9(20) Reserved
3.10(20) Informal disposition
3.11(20) Evidence of settlement negotiations

CHAPTER 4
BARGAINING UNIT AND BARGAINING REPRESENTATIVE DETERMINATION
4.1(20) General procedures
4.2(20) Unit determination
4.3(20) Bargaining representative determination (election petitions)
4.4(20) Concurrent (combined) petitions
4.5(20) Unit reconsideration
4.6(20) Amendment of unit
4.7(20) Unit clarification
4.8(20) Amendment of certification

CHAPTER 5
ELECTIONS
5.1(20) General procedures
5.2(20) Conduct of election
5.3(20) Election results—tally of ballots
5.4(20) Postelection procedures
5.5(20) Bars to an election
5.6(20) Decertification elections
5.7(20) Disclaimer
5.8(20) Destruction of ballots

CHAPTER 6
NEGOTIATIONS AND NEGOTIABILITY DISPUTES
6.1(20) Scope of negotiations
6.2(20) Consolidated negotiations
6.3(20) Negotiability disputes
6.4(20) Acceptance of proposed agreement
6.5(20) Negotiations report—filing of agreement

CHAPTER 7
IMPASSE PROCEDURES
7.1(20) General
7.2(20) Fees of neutrals
7.3(20) Mediation
7.4(20) Fact-finding
7.5(20) Binding arbitration
7.6(20) Impasse procedures after budget certification
7.7(20) Impasse procedure for state employees

CHAPTER 8
INTERNAL CONDUCT OF EMPLOYEE ORGANIZATIONS
8.1(20) Registration report
8.2(20) Annual report
8.3(20) Bonding requirements
8.4(20) Trusteeships
8.5(20) Reports as public information
8.6(20) Filing of a complaint

CHAPTER 9
ADMINISTRATIVE REMEDIES
9.1(20) Final decisions
9.2(20) Appeals to board
9.3(20) Appeals to district court

CHAPTER 10
DECLARATORY RULINGS
10.1(20) Who may petition
10.2(20) Contents of petition
10.3(17A,20) Clarifications
10.4(17A,20) Caption
10.5(17A,20) Service
10.6(17A,20) Intervention

CHAPTER 11
STATE EMPLOYEE APPEALS OF GRIEVANCE DECISIONS AND DISCIPLINARY ACTIONS
11.1(19A,20) Notice of appeal rights
11.2(19A,20) Filing of appeal
11.3(19A,20) Content of the appeal
11.4(19A,20) Content of director's answer to the appeal
11.5(19A,20) Right to a hearing
11.6(19A,20) Witnesses
11.7(19A,20) Finality of decision
11.8(19A,20) Filing of petition for review
11.9(19A,20) Other rules
11.10(19A,20) Applicability

CHAPTER 12
PUBLIC RECORDS AND FAIR INFORMATION PRACTICES
12.1(20,22) Definitions
12.2(20,22) Statement of Policy
12.3(20,22) Requests for access to records
12.4(20,22) Access to confidential records
12.5(20,22) Requests for treatment of a record as a confidential record and its withholding from examination
12.6(20,22) Procedure by which additions, dissents, or objections may be entered into certain records
12.7(20,22) Consent to disclosure by the subject of a confidential record
12.8(20,22) Notice to suppliers of information
12.9(20,22) Disclosures without the consent of the subject
12.10(20,22) Routine use
12.11(20,22) Consensual disclosure of confidential records
12.12(20,22) Release of record
12.13(20,22) Availability of records
12.14(20,22) Data processing systems
12.15(20,22) Applicability

CHAPTER 1
GENERAL PROVISIONS

621—1.1(20) Construction and severability. These rules shall be liberally construed to effectuate the purposes and provisions of the public employment relations Act. If any provisions of these rules are held to be invalid, it shall not be construed to invalidate any of the other provisions of these rules.

621—1.2(20) General agency description. The purpose of the public employment relations board established by the Public Employment Relations Act is to implement the provisions of the Act and adjudicate and conciliate employment related cases involving the state of Iowa and other public employers and employee organizations. For these purposes the powers and duties of the board include, but are not limited to, the following:

Determining appropriate bargaining units and conducting representation elections.

Adjudicating prohibited practice complaints and fashioning appropriate remedial relief for violations of the Act.

Adjudicating and serving as arbitrators regarding state merit system grievances and grievances arising under collective bargaining agreements between public employers and certified employee organizations.

Providing mediators, fact finders, and arbitrators to resolve impasse in negotiations.

Collecting and disseminating information concerning the wages, hours, and other conditions of employment of public employees.

Assisting the attorney general in the preparation of legal briefs and the presentation of oral arguments in the district court and the supreme court in cases affecting the board.

621—1.3(20) General course and method of operation. Upon receipt of a petition or complaint, the board may assign an investigator to the case to prepare a preliminary report. In the case of a complaint, the board may determine that the charge is without basis and dismiss the complaint without further proceedings. Complaints not dismissed and petitions are assigned for a hearing before either an administrative law judge or the board, unless the procedures for informal settlement described in these rules are followed. The administrative law judge or the board will conduct a hearing on the complaint or petition and issue an order. The decisions of administrative law judges are appealable to the board, and final orders and decisions of the board are appealable to the district court under the administrative procedure Act.

The board follows the procedures for adoption of rules found in the administrative procedure Act. When the board agrees to propose the adoption of a rule, the chairperson has the authority to sign and submit a notice of intended action containing the proposed rule.

621—1.4(20) Method of obtaining information and making submissions or requests. Any person may obtain information from, make submission to, or make a request of the board by writing to Chairperson, Iowa Public Employment Relations Board, 507 10th Street, Des Moines, Iowa 50309.

621—1.5(20) Petition for adoption of rules. Any person may petition the board for the adoption of a rule. Such petition shall be in writing and shall include:

1.5(1) The name and address of the person requesting the adoption of the rule;

1.5(2) A statement of the proposed rule;

1.5(3) A statement of why the rule is being proposed for adoption. Within 60 days of the board's receipt of the proposed rule, the board shall either deny the petition in writing, stating its reasons for the denial or shall initiate rule-making proceedings in accordance with Iowa Code chapter 17A.

621—1.6(20) Definitions.

1.6(1) *"Act"* as used in these rules shall mean the public employment relations Act, chapter 20.

1.6(2) *"Board"* as used in these rules shall mean the public employment relations board. No official board action may be taken without the concurrence of at least two members of the board; provided, however, that when for compelling reasons only two members hear an appeal of a recommended decision in a contested case and the two members do not concur, the result shall be affirmation of the recommended decision. The board, in its discretion, may delegate to board employees duties which the Act does not specifically require to be performed by the three member board.

1.6(3) *Petitioner—complainant—respondent—intervenor.*

a. "Petitioner" means the party filing a petition under Iowa Code section 20.13 or 20.14.

b. "Complainant" means the party filing a complaint under Iowa Code section 20.11, alleging the commission of a prohibited practice.

c. "Respondent" means the party accused of committing a prohibited practice.

d. "Intervenor" means a party who voluntarily interposes in a proceeding with the approval of the board or administrative law judge.

1.6(4) *"Party"* as used in these rules shall mean any person, employee organization or public employer who has filed a petition or complaint under the Act or these rules; who has been named as a party in a complaint, petition or other matter under these rules; or whose motion to intervene has been granted by the board.

1.6(5) *"Impasse item"* means any term which was a subject of negotiations and proposed to be included in a collective bargaining agreement upon which the parties have failed to reach agreement in the course of negotiations, except as provided for in 6.1(20). Failure of the parties to agree upon impasse procedures shall not constitute an impasse item or compel implementation of impasse procedures.

1.6(6) *"Impasse procedures"* means either the procedures set forth in Iowa Code sections 20.20, 20.21 and 20.22; or any procedures agreed upon by the parties which commence no later than 120 days prior to the certified budget submission date of the public employer, and which result in a binding collective bargaining agreement.

621—1.7(20) Computation of time. Time periods established by these rules shall be computed pursuant to Iowa Code section 4.1(22).

These rules are intended to implement Iowa Code chapter 20.

[Filed March 4, 1975]

[Filed 2/3/78, Notice 12/28/77—published 2/22/78, effective 3/29/78]

[Filed 11/7/80, Notice 9/17/80—published 11/26/80, effective 12/31/80]

[Filed 10/9/86, Notice 8/27/86—published 11/5/86, effective 12/10/86]

[Filed 2/1/89, Notice 12/28/88—published 2/22/89, effective 3/30/89]

CHAPTER 2
GENERAL PRACTICE AND HEARING PROCEDURES

621—2.1(20)   Hearing—time and place—administrative law judge. A member of the board or an administrative law judge shall fix the time and place for all hearings. Hearings may be conducted by the board, or by one or more of its members, or by an administrative law judge designated by the board. At their discretion the board or administrative law judge may order a prehearing conference.

621—2.2(20)   Notice of hearing—contents. Written notice of the hearing shall be delivered by the board to all parties by ordinary mail. The notice shall include:

2.2(1)   A statement of the time, place and nature of hearing.

2.2(2)   A statement of the legal authority and jurisdiction under which the hearing is to be held.

2.2(3)   A reference to the particular sections of the statutes and rules involved.

2.2(4)   A short and plain statement of the matters asserted.

621—2.3(20)   Failure to appear. If a party fails to appear after proper service of notice, the administrative law judge may, if no continuance is granted, proceed with the hearing and render a decision in the absence of the party.

621—2.4(20)   Intervention and additional parties. Any interested person may request intervention in any proceeding before the public employment relations board. An application for intervention shall be in writing, except that applications made during a hearing may be made orally to the hearing officer, and shall contain a statement of the reasons for such intervention. When an application for intervention is filed regarding a petition for bargaining representative determination, the rules set forth in 4.3(2), 4.4(4) and 5.1(4) shall apply.

Where necessary to achieve a more proper decision, the board or administrative law judge may, on its own motion or the motion of any party, order the bringing in of additional parties. When so ordered the board shall serve upon such additional parties all relevant pleadings, and allow such parties a reasonable time to respond thereto where appropriate.

621—2.5(20)   Continuance. Hearings or proceedings on any matter may be continued by order of the board or an administrative law judge, with the reasons therefor set out in said order, and notice thereof to all parties. Parties may, upon written application to the board prior to commencement of the hearing or other proceeding, or oral application to the administrative law judge during the hearing, but not ex parte, request a continuance. A continuance may be allowed for any cause not growing out of the fault or negligence of the applicant, which satisfies the board or administrative law judge that a proper decision or result will be more nearly obtained by granting a continuance. The continuance may also be granted if agreed to by all parties and approved by the board or administrative law judge.

621—2.6(20)   Appearances and conduct of parties. Any party may appear and be heard on its own behalf, or by its designated representative. Designated representatives shall file a notice of appearance with the board for each case in which they appear for a party. Filing of pleadings on behalf of a party shall be equivalent to filing a notice of appearance. All persons appearing in proceedings before the board shall conform to the standard of ethical conduct required of attorneys before the courts of the state of Iowa. If any person refuses to conform to such standards, the board may decline to permit such person to appear in any proceeding.

621—2.7(20) Evidence—objections. Rules of evidence shall be those set forth in the Administrative Procedure Act. Any objection with respect to the conduct of the hearing, including an objection to the introduction of evidence, may be stated orally or in writing, accompanied by a short statement of the grounds of such objection, and included in the record. No such objection shall be deemed waived by further participation in the hearing.

621—2.8(20) Order of procedure. The employer shall present its evidence first in unit determination hearings. The complainant shall present its evidence first and shall have the burden of proof in prohibited practice hearings. Intervenors shall follow the parties in whose behalf the intervention is made; if not made in support of a principal party, the administrative law judge shall designate at what stage such intervenors shall be heard. The order of other parties shall be determined by the administrative law judge. All parties shall be allowed cross-examination and an opportunity for rebuttal. At any stage of the hearing or after the close of the hearing but prior to decision, the board or administrative law judge may call for further evidence to be presented by the party or parties concerned.

621—2.9(20) Amendments. A petition, complaint or answer may be amended for good cause shown, but not ex parte, upon motion at any time prior to the decision. Allowance of such amendments, including those to conform to the proof, shall be within the discretion of the board or administrative law judge. The board or administrative law judge may impose terms, or grant a continuance with or without terms, as a condition of such allowance. Such motions prior to hearing shall be in writing filed with the board, and the moving party shall serve a copy thereof upon all parties by ordinary mail.

621—2.10(20) Briefs and arguments. At the discretion of the board or administrative law judge, oral arguments may be presented by the parties with such time limits as determined by the board or administrative law judge. Briefs may be filed in such order and within such time limits as set by the board or administrative law judge.

621—2.11(20) Sequestration of witnesses. Upon its own motion, or the motion of any party, the board or administrative law judge may order the sequestration of witnesses in any proceeding.

621—2.12(20) Subpoenas.
  2.12(1) *Attendance of witnesses.* The board, administrative law judge, or board appointed fact finder or arbitrator shall issue subpoenas to compel the attendance of witnesses and the production of relevant records upon written application of any party filed with the board prior to the hearing or oral motion at the hearing. The party requesting subpoenas shall serve the subpoenas, and notify the board in writing prior to hearing, or orally at the time of hearing, of the names and addresses of the witnesses or the person or party having possession of the requested documents. Where a subpoena has been served more than seven days prior to the hearing, a party may move to quash the subpoena not less than three days prior to the hearing. Subpoenas for production of records shall list with specificity the items sought for production and the name and address of the person or party having possession or control thereof. A motion to quash subpoenas may be filed with the board prior to hearing or with the hearing officer, fact finder or arbitrator at the time of hearing. The motion filed prior to hearing shall be in writing, and the moving party shall provide copies to all parties of record.

2.12(2) *Witness fees.* Witnesses shall receive from the subpoenaing party fees and expenses as are prescribed by statute for witnesses in civil actions before a district court. Witnesses may, however, waive such fees and expenses.

2.12(3) *Service of subpoenas.* Subpoenas shall be served as provided in Iowa Code section 622.63.

621—2.13(20) Form of documents. All documents, other than forms provided by the board, which relate to any proceeding before the board should be typewritten and bear the docket number of the proceeding to which it relates. Such documents may be single or double-spaced at the option of the submitting party.

621—2.14(20) Captions. The following captions for documents other than forms provided by the board are suggested for use in practice before the board:

2.14(1) In prohibited practice proceedings:
Before the Public Employment Relations Board

XYZ,
   Complainant

                                 [name of document]

and

                                 Case No. 1234

J. Doe,
   Respondent

2.14(2) In proceedings pursuant to a petition:
Before the Public Employment Relations Board

In the matter of

XYZ,
   Public Employer
                                 [name of document]

and

                                 Case No. 1234

J. Doe, Petitioner

621—2.15(20) Service of pleadings and other papers.

2.15(1) *Service—upon whom made.* Whenever under these rules service is required to be made upon a party, such service shall be as follows:

   a. Upon any city, or board, commission, council or agency thereof, by serving the mayor or city clerk.

   b. Upon any county, or office, board, commission or agency thereof, by serving the county auditor or the chairperson of the county board of supervisors.

   c. Upon any school district, school township, or school corporation by serving the presiding officer or secretary of its governing body.

   d. Upon the state of Iowa, or board, commission, council, office or agency thereof, by serving the governor or the director of personnel.

   e. Upon the state judicial department by serving the state court administrator.

   f. Upon any other governing body by serving its presiding officer, clerk or secretary.

g. Upon an employee organization by serving the person designated by the employee organization to receive service pursuant to 8.2(2), or, by service upon the president or secretary of the employee organization.

h. Upon any other person by serving that person or his or her attorney of record.

2.15(2) *Service—how made.* Except as provided in rules 3.4(20) and 5.7(20) and subrules 2.12(3) and 4.2(2), whenever these rules require service upon any person or party the service shall be sufficient if made by ordinary mail.

2.15(3) *Proof of service.* Where service is by restricted certified mail or personal service, the serving party shall forward the return receipt or return of service to the board for filing. Where service by ordinary mail is permitted under these rules, the serving party shall include the following certificate on the original document filed with the board:

"I hereby certify that on _____ I sent a copy of the fore-

(date)

going matter to the following parties of record or their representatives at the addresses indicated, by depositing same in a United States mail receptacle with sufficient postage affixed.

(Signed) _____ "

(party or representative)

621—2.16(20) Consolidation. Upon application of any party or upon its own motion, the board or an administrative law judge, may consolidate for hearing any cases which involve common questions of law or fact.

621—2.17(20) Prohibition against testimony of mediators, fact finders, arbitrators and board employees. A mediator, fact finder, arbitrator, labor relations examiner, administrative law judge, member of the board or other officer or employee of the board shall not testify on behalf of any party to a prohibited practice, representation or impasse resolution proceeding, pending in any court or before the board, with respect to any information, facts, or other matter coming to that individual's knowledge through a party or parties in an official capacity as a resolver of disputes.

621—2.18(20) Delivery of decisions and orders. Decisions and orders of the board or administrative law judge shall be delivered to the parties by ordinary mail.

621—2.19(20) Stays of agency action. Application for stays of agency actions must be filed with the board and served upon all interested parties pursuant to rule 2.15(20). The board may in its discretion and on such terms as it deems proper, grant or deny an application.

621—2.20(20) Ex parte communications.

2.20(1) *Communications prohibited.* Unless required for the disposition of ex parte matters specifically authorized by statute, an individual assigned to render a proposed or final decision or to make findings of fact or conclusions of law in a contested case, or a declaratory ruling in which there are two or more parties, shall not communicate directly or indirectly with any person or party, nor shall such person or party communicate directly or indirectly with such an individual concerning any issues of fact or law pending in that case, unless each party or its representative is given prior written notice of the communication. Such notice shall contain a summary of the communication, if oral, or a copy of the communication if written, and the time, place and means of such communication.

2.20(2) *Disclosure of prohibited communications.* Any communication between a party and an individual assigned to render a proposed or final decision, or to make findings of fact or conclusions of law in a contested case, or a declaratory ruling where there are two or more parties, which is made under circumstances and procedures which do not substantially comply with those set forth in subrule 2.20(1) is a prohibited communication. The recipient of a prohibited communication is required to submit the communication if written, or a summary of the communication if oral, for inclusion in the record of the case proceeding. After such submission, all parties shall have the right, upon written demand, to respond to such communication.

2.20(3) *Penalty for prohibited communications.*

a. The penalty for making a prohibited communication may be censure, suspension, or revocation of the privilege to practice before the board in the case of a party or their representative; and censure, suspension, or dismissal in the case of agency personnel.

b. The censure, suspension or revocation of a person's right to practice before the board due to an alleged violation of the prohibition against ex parte communications shall constitute a contested case as that term is defined in Iowa Code section 17A.2 and no person shall be censured or the right to practice before the board be suspended or revoked without notice and an opportunity to be heard as provided in Iowa Code chapter 17A, "The Iowa Administrative Procedure Act."

621—2.21(20)   Transcripts of record. Testimony in all hearings before the board shall be taken by a certified shorthand reporter or, unless a party objects, by other mechanized means. The board does not furnish copies of transcriptions, but recorded proceedings shall be transcribed at the expense of any party requesting the transcription. Arguments on motions, oral arguments on appeal to the board, and arguments made in declaratory ruling and expedited negotiability dispute proceedings, need not be recorded.

621—2.22(20)   Dismissal. The board or an administrative law judge may dismiss cases for want of prosecution if, after receiving notice by certified mail, the parties do not show good cause why the case should be retained.

These rules are intended to implement Iowa Code chapter 20.

[Filed 3/4/75]
|Filed 10/29/76, Notice 9/22/76—published 11/17/76, effective 12/22/76|
|Filed 10/26/77, Notice 9/21/77—published 11/16/77, effective 12/21/77|
[Filed 2/3/78, Notice 12/28/77—published 2/22/78, effective 3/29/78]
[Filed 11/7/80, Notice 9/17/80—published 11/26/80, effective 12/31/80]
[Filed 10/22/82, Notice 9/15/82—published 11/10/82, effective 12/15/82]
[Filed emergency 7/23/85—published 8/14/85, effective 7/23/85]
[Filed 10/9/86, Notice 8/27/86—published 11/5/86, effective 12/10/86]
[Filed 2/1/89, Notice 12/28/88—published 2/22/89, effective 3/30/89]

CHAPTER 3
PROHIBITED PRACTICE COMPLAINTS

621—3.1(20) Filing of complaint. A complaint that any person, organization, or public employer has engaged in or is engaging in a prohibited practice under the Act may be filed by any person, employee organization or public employer. A complaint shall be in writing and signed according to these rules, and may be on a form provided by the board. The complaint shall be filed with the board. A complaint shall be deemed untimely and shall be dismissed if filed with the board more than ninety (90) days following the alleged violation.

621—3.2(20) Contents of complaint. The complaint shall include the following:

3.2(1) The name and address and organizational affiliation, if any, of the complainant, and the title of any representative filing the complaint.

3.2(2) The name and address of the respondent or respondents and any other party named therein.

3.2(3) A clear and concise statement of the facts constituting the alleged prohibited practice, including the names of the individuals involved in the alleged act, the dates and places of the alleged occurrence, and the specific section or sections of the Act alleged to have been violated.

621—3.3(20)   Clarification of complaint. The board may, on its own motion or motion of the respondent, require the complainant to make the complaint more specific in certain particulars.

621—3.4(20)   Service of complaint. The complainant shall serve the respondent(s) with a copy of the complaint in the manner of an original notice or by restricted certified mail, return receipt requested, addressed to the last known address of the respondent(s). Service shall be upon the person designated for service by subrule 2.15(1). The service shall be made within ten days of the filing of the complaint with the board, and the complainant shall file the return of service with the board.

621—3.5(20)   Answer to complaint.
   3.5(1) *Filing and service.* Within ten days of service of a complaint, the respondent(s) shall file with the board a written answer to the complaint, and cause a copy to be delivered to the complainant by ordinary mail to the address set forth in the complaint. The answer shall be signed by the respondent(s) or the designated representative of the respondent(s).
   3.5(2) *Extension of time to answer.* Upon application and good cause shown, the board may extend the time to answer to a time and date certain.
   3.5(3) *Contents of answer.* The answer shall include a specific admission or denial of each allegation of the complaint or, if the respondent is without knowledge thereof, the respondent shall so state and such statement shall operate as a denial. Admissions or denials may be made to all or part of an allegation, but shall fairly meet the circumstances of the allegations. Where matters are denied with knowledge, the respondent shall set forth the specific facts as known to the respondent with regard to such matters. The answer shall include a specific detailed statement of any affirmative defense. Matters contained in the answer shall be deemed to have been denied by the complaint, and no responsive pleading is required.
   3.5(4) *Admission by failure to answer.* If the respondent fails to file a timely answer, such failure may be deemed by the board to constitute an admission of the material facts alleged in the complaint and a waiver by the respondent of a hearing.

621—3.6(20)   Withdrawal of complaint. A complaint or any part thereof may be withdrawn with the consent of the board, and upon conditions the board may deem proper. Withdrawal shall constitute a bar to refiling the same complaint or part thereof by the complainant.

621—3.7(20)   Amendment of complaint or answer. See 2.9(20).

621—3.8(20)   Investigation of complaint. Subsequent to the filing of a complaint, the board or its designee may conduct a preliminary investigation of the allegations of the complaint. In conducting such investigation, the board may require the complainant and respondent to furnish evidence, including affidavits and other documents if appropriate. If a review of the evidence shows that the complaint has no basis in fact, the complaint shall be dismissed with prejudice by order of the board and the parties notified. Board employees involved in investigations under this section shall not act as administrative law judges in any proceeding related to the investigation.
   3.9 Rescinded, effective December 22, 1976.

621—3.10(20)   Informal disposition. Any party seeking to settle a controversy which may result in a contested case may request assistance from the board. The board may schedule meetings between the parties and assist the parties to reach a settlement of the dispute; provided, however, that no party shall be required to participate in informal settlement attempts or to settle the controversy pursuant to this section. Any prohibited practice case commenced with the board may be informally settled by stipulation, agreed settlement, consent order, default, or by any other method agreed upon by the parties in writing, subject, however, to approval by the board.

621—3.11(20) Evidence of settlement negotiations. Evidence of proposed offers of settlement of a prohibited practice complaint shall be inadmissible at the hearing thereon.
These rules are intended to implement Iowa Code chapter 20.

[Filed 3/4/75]
[Filed 10/29/76, Notice 9/22/76—published 11/17/76, effective 12/22/76]
|Filed 10/26/77, Notice 9/21/77—published 11/16/77, effective 12/21/77|
[Filed 11/7/80, Notice 9/17/80—published 11/26/80, effective 12/31/80]
[Filed emergency 7/23/85—published 8/14/85, effective 7/23/85]
[Filed 10/9/86, Notice 8/27/86—published 11/5/86, effective 12/10/86]
[Filed 2/1/89, Notice 12/28/88—published 2/22/89, effective 3/30/89]

CHAPTER 4
BARGAINING UNIT AND BARGAINING
REPRESENTATIVE DETERMINATION

621—4.1(20) General procedures.
4.1(1) *Separate or combined petitions.* Request for bargaining unit determination and bargaining representative determination shall be by petitions which may be filed separately. Where a request has been made to a public employer to bargain collectively with a designated group of public employees and the board has not previously determined the bargaining unit, the petitions shall be filed jointly or on a combined form provided by the board.
4.1(2) *Intervention and additional parties.* See rule 2.4(20).
4.1(3) *Withdrawal of petitions.* Petitions may be withdrawn only with the consent of the board. Petitions withdrawn after the commencement of a hearing, or withdrawn after direction of an election where no hearing was conducted, may not be refiled by the withdrawing party for a period of six months following the board order permitting withdrawal.

621—4.2(20) Unit determination.
4.2(1) *Content of petition.* A petition for bargaining unit determination shall be on a form provided by the board and shall be filed by delivery to the board. The petition shall contain an identification and description of the proposed unit.
4.2(2) *Notice to parties.* Upon receipt of a proper petition, the board shall serve copies thereof upon other interested parties by certified mail, return receipt requested. Upon the filing of a petition for unit determination, the board shall furnish to the employer a notice to employees, giving notice that the petition has been filed and setting forth the rights of employees under the Act. Notices shall be posted by the public employer in conspicuous places customarily used for the posting of notices to employees.
4.2(3) *Notice of hearing.* The board or administrative law judge shall issue a notice of hearing by ordinary mail to all interested parties setting forth the time, date and place of the hearing and any other relevant information. The board or administrative law judge shall provide additional copies of the notice of hearing to the public employer, which shall be posted by the public employer in conspicuous places customarily used for the posting of information to employees.
4.2(4) *Intervention.* See rule 2.4(20).
4.2(5) *Professional and nonprofessional elections.* If, in any case, the board should determine that professional employees and nonprofessional employees could be represented in a single bargaining unit, the board shall direct and supervise an election among such employees to determine whether they wish to be represented in a single or in separate

bargaining units. The election shall be by secret ballot under conditions as the board may prescribe. Absentee ballots shall be as provided for in 5.2(5). The elections may, in the discretion of the board, be conducted in whole or in part by mail ballots provided for in 5.1(3). A majority affirmative vote of those voting in each category shall be necessary to include professional and nonprofessional employees within the same bargaining unit. The rules concerning voting lists, as set forth in 5.1(2), shall apply.

4.2(6) *Informal settlement of bargaining unit determination.* Cases on bargaining unit determination may be informally settled in the following manner:

a. The petitioning party shall prepare a stipulation setting forth in detail the composition of the bargaining unit as agreed upon by all parties. The stipulation shall be signed by the authorized representative of the parties involved and shall be forwarded to the board for informal review and tentative approval. In the event the parties agree to a combined unit of professional and nonprofessional employees, the stipulation shall set forth both those job classifications included within the professional category and those job classifications included within the nonprofessional category. If the board fails to tentatively approve the stipulation, the board shall notify the parties and, unless the parties amend the stipulation in a manner to gain tentative approval of the board, the matter shall proceed to hearing. If the board tentatively approves the stipulation, the board shall prepare a public notice of proposed decision and shall deliver copies to the parties. The public employer shall post the notice of the proposed decision, for a period of not less than one calendar week, in a prominent place in the main office of the public employer accessible to the general public and in conspicuous places customarily used for the posting of information to employees. The public employer shall also have copies of the proposed decision available for distribution to the public upon request.

b. Notice of the proposed decision shall be on a form provided by the board which shall identify the parties; specify the terms of the proposed decision; list the names, addresses and telephone numbers of the parties or their authorized representatives to whom inquiries by the public should be directed; and, further, state the date by which written objection to the proposed decision must be filed with the board and the address to which such objections should be sent.

c. Objections to the proposed decision must be filed with the board by the date posted in the notice of proposed decision. Objections shall be in writing and shall set out the specific grounds of objection. The objecting party must identify itself and provide a mailing address and telephone number. The board shall promptly advise the parties of the objections and make any investigation deemed appropriate. If the board deems the objections to be of substance, the parties may, with board approval, amend their proposed decision to conform therewith, and the objecting party shall be notified by the board of the amendment. If the objections cannot be informally resolved, they may be dismissed or resolved at hearing.

d. Final board decision on the informed settlement shall be reserved until expiration of the time for filing of objections. If no objections have been filed; or if filed objections have been resolved through amendment of the proposed decision; or if filed objections, after inquiry by the board, were found to be frivolous, the board shall endorse the proposed decision as final.

e. If interested parties are unable to informally settle a case on bargaining unit determination within fifteen days of service of a petition, the board or administrative law judge may order any interested party to file with the board its proposed unit description.

621—4.3(20) Bargaining representative determination (election petitions).

4.3(1) *Form of petition.* A petition for bargaining representative determination (election petition) shall be on a form provided by the board and shall be filed by delivery to the board. These petitions shall be of three types:

a. A certification petition, filed by an employee organization requesting that through an election it be certified as the exclusive bargaining representative in an appropriate unit of public employees. The name of the employee organization which appears on the petition, or the petition as amended, shall be the name which appears on the election ballot.

b. A decertification petition, filed by an employee requesting an election to determine whether a certified bargaining representative does, in fact, represent a majority of the employees in the bargaining unit, and

c. A representation petition, filed by a public employer requesting an election to determine the bargaining representative, if any, of the employees in the bargaining unit.

4.3(2) *Showing of interest—certification—decertification—intervention.* Whenever a petition for certification or decertification is filed, or whenever intervention is requested for the purpose of being placed on an election ballot, the petitioner or intervenor shall submit therewith evidence that the petition or application for intervention is supported by employees in the unit in the following percentages: Thirty percent (30%) for certification or decertification and ten percent (10%) for intervention in election proceedings. In petitions for certification or applications for intervention, such interest showing shall be dated and signed not more than one year prior to its submission; shall contain the job classification of the signator; and shall contain a statement that the signator is a member of the employee organization or has authorized it to bargain collectively on the signatory's behalf. In appropriate cases, an authenticated dues checkoff list may be used for this purpose. In petitions for decertification, evidence of interest shall be as provided above and shall further contain a statement that the signator no longer wishes to be represented by the certified employee organization. When a representation petition is filed by an employer, no show of interest will be required.

4.3(3) *Determination of showing of interest.* The public employer shall, within seven (7) days of receipt of notice of a certification petition, submit to the board a list of the names and job classifications of the employees in the unit requested by the petitioner. The board shall administratively determine the sufficiency of the showing of interest upon receipt of the list. This determination, including the identification and number of signers of the showing of interest, shall be confidential and not subject to review, and parties other than the party submitting the interest showing shall not be entitled to a copy or examination of the showing of interest. If the employer fails to furnish the list of employees, the board shall determine the sufficiency of the showing of interest by whatever means it deems appropriate. In election proceedings where the petitioner withdraws its petition pursuant to subrule 4.1(3), in the presence of an intervenor, the election shall not be conducted unless the intervenor produces a thirty percent (30%) showing of interest within a time period determined by the board.

4.3(4) *Notice.* Upon the filing of a petition for certification, decertification or representation, the board shall furnish to the employer a notice to employees, giving notice to employees that an election petition has been filed and setting forth the rights of employees under the Act. Such notices shall be posted by the public employer in conspicuous places customarily used for the posting of information to employees.

4.3(5) *Direction of election.* Whenever an election petition is filed which conforms to these rules and the Act and the appropriate bargaining unit has been previously determined, an election shall be directed and conducted.

4.3(6) *Intervention.* See 4.1(2).

621—4.4(20) Concurrent (combined) petitions.

4.4(1) *When to file.* A combined petition for both bargaining unit determination and bargaining representative determination shall be filed whenever a question of representation exists and the bargaining unit has not been previously determined by the board.

4.4(2) *Content of petition.* A combined petition for unit determination and representative determination (election) shall be on a form provided by the board and shall be filed by delivery to the board.

4.4(3) *Notice of petition, hearing, and notice to employees.* Upon receipt of a combined petition, notice shall be as provided in 4.2(2), 4.2(3) and 4.3(4).

4.4(4) *Showing of interest.* Showing of interest shall be as provided in 4.3(2) and 4.3(3). Should the board determine an appropriate unit different than that requested, any employee organization affected may request a reasonable period of time to submit additional evidence of interest sufficient to satisfy the requirements of the Act.

4.4(5) *Scope of hearing.* Hearings on combined petitions shall resolve all issues with regard to both bargaining unit determination and bargaining representative determination.

4.4(6) *Intervention.* See 4.1(2).

4.4(7) *Professional and nonprofessional elections.* See 4.2(5).

621—4.5(20) **Unit reconsideration.** A petition for reconsideration of a board-established bargaining unit may be filed by an employee organization, public employer, or an employee of the public employer. This petition may be filed only in combination with an election petition. The rules set forth in 4.1(20), 4.2(20), 4.3(20) and 4.4(20) shall apply, except that the board may investigate the petition and, if it determines that the petitioner has not established grounds that the previous board determination of the bargaining unit is inappropriate, the board may dismiss the petition. A petition for reconsideration of a board-established bargaining unit covering state employees may not be filed until after one year of the initial unit determination.

621—4.6(20) **Amendment of unit.**

4.6(1) *Petition.* A petition for amendment of a board determined bargaining unit may be filed by the public employer or the certified employee organization. The petition shall contain:

a. Name and address of the public employer and the employee organization.

b. An identification and description of the proposed amended unit.

c. The names and addresses of any other employee organizations which claim to represent any employees affected by the proposed amendment or a statement that the petitioner has no knowledge of any other such organization.

d. Job classifications of the employees as to whom the issue is raised and the number of employees, if any, in each classification.

e. A specific statement of the petitioner's reasons for seeking amendment of the unit and any other relevant facts.

4.6(2) *Procedure—decision.* Insofar as applicable, the rules set forth in 4.2(20) shall apply, except that the board may conduct an investigation and issue a decision and order without hearing.

4.6(3) *Elections; when required.* A question of representation exists, and the board will conduct a representation election, if the job classification(s) sought to be amended into a bargaining unit was in existence at the time the employee organization was certified to represent the bargaining unit and the job classification(s) separately constitutes an appropriate bargaining unit.

621—4.7(20) **Unit clarification.** A petition to clarify the inclusion or exclusion of job classifications or employees in a board determined bargaining unit may be filed by the public employer, an affected public employee, or the certified employee organization. Such petition must be in the absence of a question of representation. Insofar as applicable, the procedures for such filing shall be as provided in subrules 4.6(1) and 4.6(2).

621—4.8(20) **Amendment of certification.**

4.8(1) *Name changes—merger—affiliation—disaffiliation.* Petitions for amendment of certification to reflect changes in the certification resulting from a name change, merger, affiliation, or disaffiliation must be accompanied by an affidavit stating that the merger, affiliation, or disaffiliation was authorized by, and accomplished in accordance with the certified employee organization's constitution and bylaws.

4.8(2) When a petition for amendment of certification is filed under 4.8(1) or under 4.8(2), the board shall mail copies of a public notice of proposed decision to the parties. The public employer shall post the notice of proposed decision, for a period of not less than one calendar week, in a prominent place in the main office of the public employer accessible to the general public and in conspicuous places customarily used for the posting of information to employees.

The public employer shall also have copies of the proposed decision available for distribution to the public upon request.

a. Notice of the proposed decision shall be on a form provided by the board which shall identify the parties; specify the terms of the proposed decision; list the names, addresses and telephone numbers of the parties or their authorized representatives to whom inquiries by the public should be directed; and, further, state the date by which written objection to the proposed decision must be filed with the board and the address to which the objections should be sent.

b. Objections to the proposed decision must be filed with the board by the date posted in the notice of proposed decision. Objections shall be in writing and shall set out the specific grounds of objection. The objecting party must identify itself and provide a mailing address and telephone number. The board shall promptly advise the parties of the objections and make any investigation deemed appropriate. When an objection is raised the board may investigate and dismiss the objection or conduct a hearing pursuant to chapter 2 of these rules and regulations.

c. Final board decision shall be reserved until expiration of the time for filing objections. If no objections have been filed, the board may endorse the proposed decision as final.

These rules are intended to implement Iowa Code chapter 20.

[Filed 3/4/75]
[Filed 10/29/76, Notice 9/22/76—published 11/17/76, effective 12/22/76]
[Filed 10/26/77, Notice 9/21/77—published 11/16/77, effective 12/21/77]
[Filed 9/11/79, Notice 7/11/79—published 10/3/79, effective 11/12/79]
[Filed 11/7/80, Notice 9/17/80—published 11/26/80, effective 12/31/80]
[Filed emergency 7/23/85—published 8/14/85, effective 7/23/85]
[Filed 10/9/86, Notice 8/27/86—published 11/5/86, effective 12/10/86]
[Filed 2/1/89, Notice 12/28/88—published 2/22/89, effective 3/30/89]

CHAPTER 5
ELECTIONS

621—5.1(20) General procedures.

5.1(1) *Notice of election.* Upon direction of an election, notices of election, in a form provided by the board, shall be posted by the public employer in conspicuous places customarily used for the posting of information to employees. Such notices shall contain a sample ballot and shall set forth the date, time, place and purpose of the election, and such additional information as the board may deem appropriate.

5.1(2) *Eligibility—eligibility list.* Eligible voters are those employees who:

a. Were employed in the bargaining unit during the payroll period immediately preceding the direction of election unless another date is agreed upon by the parties and the board, and

b. Are employed in the bargaining unit on the date of the election. When the election is conducted in whole or in part by mail ballot or is conducted on more than one date, the date of the election shall be the date on which the ballots are to be counted. Where the board issues an order defining the appropriate bargaining unit and an election petition is pending, or in the case of a combined petition, the board shall further order the public employer to submit to the board within seven (7) days an alphabetical list of the names, addresses and job classifications of the employees in the appropriate unit. Where such a list has previously been submitted to the board, it may be utilized under this rule; provided that additions or deletions of employees, changes in address or job classifications, or other changes shall be submitted to the board to reflect the current status of employees in the bargaining unit. The list required by this rule shall be provided by the board to all parties at least ten (10) days prior to the date of the election and shall become the official voting list for any election conducted. The list may further be amended by agreement of the parties immediately prior to the election. In the case of a combined professional and nonprofessional unit, the public employer shall submit lists of employees in the professional category and employees in the nonprofessional category.

5.1(3) *Mail ballots.* The board may, in its discretion, conduct an election in whole or in part by mail ballot. In such cases, the board shall send by ordinary mail an official ballot and a postpaid return-addressed secret envelope to each eligible voter and direct a date by which voted ballots must be received by the board to be counted. The board shall also set a time and place for the counting of such ballots, at which time the parties to the election shall be entitled to be present and challenge for good cause the eligibility of any voter. Mail ballots sent to eligible voters shall consist of a ballot, a secret envelope in which said ballot is to be inserted, and an outer envelope for mailing said ballot and identification of voter for purposes of proposing challenges to his or her eligibility. In the event of a challenge, both envelopes shall remain sealed until such time as the challenge is resolved. In the event of no challenge, the mailing envelope shall be opened and the envelope containing the secret ballot shall be deposited in the ballot box.

5.1(4) *Time for intervention.* No employee organization may be placed on any ballot unless application for intervention, as provided in 4.1(2), is received by the board within seven (7) calendar days after the direction of an election. Submission of an adequate showing of interest, as provided in 4.3(2), must be received by the board within seven (7) calendar days after the direction of the election, unless an extension of time, upon written request, is granted by the board.

5.1(5) *Withdrawal from ballot.* An employee organization may, upon its request, be removed from any ballot with the approval of the board.

621—5.2(20) Conduct of election.

5.2(1) *General procedure—ballots.* After consulting with the parties to an election the board shall determine the date, place, and other procedural aspects of conducting the election. Elections shall be conducted under the direction and supervision of the board or its election agent and shall be by secret ballot. Ballots shall be provided by the board and shall contain the question required by Iowa Code section 20.15. The question in an election where only one employee organization appears on the ballot shall ask, "Do you wish to be represented for purposes of collective bargaining by [name of employee organization]?", followed by the choices "Yes" or "No"; the question in an election where more than one employee organization appears on the ballot shall state: "Do you wish to be represented for purposes of collective bargaining by:" and shall then list horizontally or vertically thereafter the choices available, including the name of each employee organization and the choice of "Neither" or "No Representative", as is applicable. In decertification elections, ballots shall be provided by the board and shall ask: "Do you desire that [name of certified employee organization] be decertified by the Public Employment Relations Board and cease to be your exclusive bargaining representative?", followed by the choices "Yes" or "No".

5.2(2) *Observers.* The parties to an election may each designate an equal number of representatives, not to exceed one (1) per voting site, to act as its observers during the election and tally of ballots. Unless agreed to by the parties observers shall not be supervisory employees of the public employer.

5.2(3) *Ballot box.* Upon examination by the observers and prior to the opening of the polls, the election agent shall seal the ballot box so that entry thereto is limited to one slot. In the event that the election is continued for more than one polling period or at more than one polling place, the ballot box shall be sealed in its entirety and shall remain in the custody of the election agent until immediately prior to the next polling period or the counting of the ballots.

5.2(4) *Voting procedure—challenges.* An eligible voter shall cast the ballot by marking the voter's choice(s) on the ballot and depositing it in the ballot box. If a voter inadvertently spoils a ballot, the ballot may be returned to the agent, who shall void and retain it and deliver to the voter another ballot. When a voter is unable to mark the ballot due to physical disability or inability to read or write, the agent may privately assist the voter.

An authorized observer or the board's election agent may challenge for good cause the eligibility of any voter, provided such challenge is made prior to the time the voter casts the ballot. The challenged voter may mark the ballot in secret and the election agent shall segregate the ballot by causing it to be placed in the envelope with appropriate markings and deposited in the ballot box.

5.2(5) *Absentee ballot.* An absentee ballot shall be delivered to an eligible voter only upon the voter's written notice to the board of the voter's inability to be present at the election for good cause. The voted ballot must be in the possession of the election agent prior to the close of the manual election in order to be counted and shall be in the official envelope provided for this purpose. Challenges to the eligibility of absentee voters may be made at the time the ballots are commingled.

621—5.3(20) Election results—tally of ballots. At the close of the polls, or at time and place as the board may prescribe, the election agent shall open the ballot box and tabulate the results of the election. Void ballots shall be those which do not indicate the clear intent of the voter or which appear to identify the voter.

621—5.4(20) Postelection procedures.

5.4(1) *Certification of results.*

a. Upon completion of a valid representation certification election in which an employee organization received the votes of a majority of those employees voting, the board shall certify that employee organization as the exclusive bargaining representative of the employees in the bargaining unit.

b. Upon completion of a valid representation certification election in which only one (1) employee organization appeared on the ballot and that employee organization did not receive the votes of a majority of those voting, the board shall serve notice of noncertification.

c. Upon completion of a valid election in which more than one (1) employee organization appeared on the ballot and no choice on the ballot received the votes of a majority of those employees voting, the board shall conduct a runoff election between the two (2) choices receiving the greatest number of votes. If the runoff election is held less than thirty (30) days after the original election, those eligible to vote shall be those who were eligible to vote in the original election and are still employed in the bargaining unit on the day of the runoff election. If the runoff election is held more than thirty (30) days after the original election, the board may direct the employer to submit a new eligibility list based upon a revised voter eligibility date.

d. Upon completion of a valid election, as provided for in paragraph "*c*" above, the board shall certify as the exclusive bargaining representative the employee organization receiving the votes of a majority of those employees voting; if no employee organization on the runoff ballot receives a majority of the votes of those employees voting, the board shall serve notice of noncertification.

e. If an employee organization fails to comply with the provisions of Iowa Code section 20.25 within ninety (90) days of the completion of a valid election, the board shall serve notice of noncertification; provided, however, that extensions of time to comply may be granted by the board upon good cause shown.

f. Upon completion of a valid decertification election, in which a majority of employees voting cast their ballots in the affirmative, the board shall serve notice of decertification.

g. Upon completion of a valid decertification election, in which a majority of employees voting cast their ballots in the negative, or in the case of a tie, the board shall serve notice of continued certification.

5.4(2) *Challenged ballots; objections.* Whenever challenged ballots are determinative of the outcome of an election or timely objections are filed, a hearing shall be scheduled. Objections to an election must be filed within ten (10) days of service of the tally of ballots on the parties, even when challenged ballots are determinative of the outcome of the election, and must contain a statement of facts upon which the objections are based. The objections shall be filed with the board and a copy shall be served upon each of the other parties to the election, with certificate of service endorsed upon the original filed with the board.

5.4(3) *Objectionable conduct during election campaigns.* The following types of activity, if conducted during the period beginning with the filing of an election petition with the board and ending at the conclusion of the election, and if determined by the board that such activity could have affected the results of the election, shall be considered to be objectionable conduct sufficient to invalidate the results of an election:

a. Electioneering within three hundred (300) feet or within sound of the polling place established by the board during the conduct of the election;

b. Misstatements of material facts by any party to the election or its representative without sufficient time for the adversely affected party to adequately respond;

c. Any misuse of board documents, including an indication that the board endorses any particular choice appearing on the ballot;

d. Campaign speeches to assembled groups of employees during working hours within the twenty-four (24)-hour period before the election;

e. Any polling of employees by a public employer which relates to the employees' preference for or against a bargaining representative;

f. Commission of a prohibited practice;

g. Any other misconduct or other circumstance which prevents employees from freely expressing their preferences in the election.

621—5.5(20)   Bars to an election. Notwithstanding the filing or pendency of an election petition, the board shall conduct no representation election when one or more of the following conditions exist:

5.5(1)   During the one (1)-year period following the date of certification or noncertification subsequent to a valid representation election.

5.5(2)   In any case where the board determines that substantial changes in the employer's operations are occurring which will imminently and substantially alter the structure or scope of the bargaining unit.

5.5(3)   Whenever a collective bargaining agreement exists, provided such agreement is written and executed by the parties to it; that such agreement is between a public employer and a certified employee organization; that such agreement does not discriminate among groups of employees on the basis of age, race, sex, religion, national origin or physical disability, as provided by law; and provided further, that any such agreement which exists for a duration in excess of two (2) years shall be deemed for the purposes of this section to be for a duration of two (2) years only. This contract bar shall not apply to a representation election in an amendment of unit case.

621—5.6(20)   Decertification elections. Petitions for decertification which are filed with the board not less than one hundred eighty (180) nor more than two hundred forty (240) days prior to the expiration of an otherwise valid collective bargaining agreement shall be processed by the board notwithstanding the provisions of 5.5(3), and the board shall, pursuant to Iowa Code section 20.15, conduct an election not more than one hundred eighty (180) nor less than one hundred fifty (150) days prior to the expiration of the collective bargaining agreement.

621—5.7(20)   Disclaimer. Notwithstanding the provisions of rule 5.6(20), the board will process a valid decertification petition accompanied by an adequate show of interest as required by subrule 4.3(2) at any time if the certified employee organization files a disclaimer of representation. A disclaimer of representation is a statement signed by an authorized representative of the certified employee organization, stating that the employee organization wishes to disclaim representation of the employees in the certified bargaining unit.

a. Upon receipt of a disclaimer and a valid petition for decertification, the board shall serve copies of the disclaimer and petition upon the employer by certified mail. The board shall prepare a public notice of proposed decision that the employee organization will be decertified and cease to be the certified representative of the employees in the bargaining unit. The public employer shall post the notice of the proposed decertification for a period of not less than one (1) calendar week in a prominent place in the main office of the public employer accessible to the general public and in conspicuous places customarily used for the posting of information to employees. The public employer shall also have copies of the proposed decertification available for distribution to the public upon request.

b. Notice of the proposed decertification shall be on a form provided by the board which shall identify the parties; specify that the employee organization seeks to disclaim representation; specify the unit currently represented by the employee organization; list the names, addresses, and telephone numbers of the parties or their authorized representatives to whom inquiries by the public should be directed; and state the date by which written objection to the proposed decertification must be filed with the board and the address to which the objections should be sent.

c. Objections to the proposed decertification must be filed with the board by the date posted in the notice. Objections shall be in writing and shall set out the specific grounds for objection. The objecting party must be identified and provide a mailing address and telephone number. The board shall promptly advise the parties of the objections. If the objections cannot be informally resolved, they shall be resolved at hearing or the board may direct and conduct a decertification election pursuant to rule 5.6(20).

d. If no objections have been filed, or if filed and the board has determined that the objections lack substance, the board shall order the decertification of the employee organization for the unit specified. If the employee organization is decertified pursuant to this rule, no representation election involving the same employee organization and the same unit may be conducted for a period of one (1) year from the date of decertification.

621—5.8(20) Destruction of ballots. In the absence of litigation over the validity or outcome of an election and after a period of sixty (60) days has elapsed from the date of the certification, decertification, or noncertification of an employee organization pursuant to a certification or decertification election, the board may destroy the ballots involved in such election.

These rules are intended to implement Iowa Code chapter 20. [Rules 5.2 and 5.4 implement Iowa Code section 20.15]

[Filed 3/4/75]
[Filed 10/29/76, Notice 9/22/76—published 11/17/76, effective 12/22/76]
[Filed emergency 7/22/77—published 8/10/77, effective 8/15/77]
[Filed 10/26/77, Notice 9/21/77—published 11/16/77, effective 12/21/77]
[Filed 11/7/80, Notice 9/17/80—published 11/26/80, effective 12/31/80]
[Filed 10/22/82, Notice 9/15/82—published 11/10/82, effecitve 12/15/82]
[Filed emergency 7/23/85—published 8/14/85, effective 7/23/85]
[Filed 10/9/86, Notice 8/27/86—published 11/5/86, effective 12/10/86]

CHAPTER 6
NEGOTIATIONS AND NEGOTIABILITY DISPUTES

621—6.1(20) Scope of negotiations. The scope of negotiations shall be as provided in section nine of the Act. Either party may introduce other matters for negotiation, and negotiation on these matters may continue until resolved by mutual agreement of the parties or until negotiations reach the fact-finding or arbitration stage of impasse; provided, however, that no party may be required to negotiate on nonmandatory subjects of bargaining. Unresolved other matters shall be excluded from the fact-finding or arbitration processes unless submission has been mutually agreed upon by the parties. The agreement is applicable only to negotiations toward the collective bargaining agreement then sought and is not binding upon the parties for future negotiations.

621—6.2(20) Consolidated negotiations. Nothing in these rules shall prohibit, by agreement of the parties, more than one certified bargaining representative from bargaining jointly with a common public employer, or more than one public employer from bargaining jointly with a common certified bargaining representative, or any other combination thereof.

621—6.3(20) Negotiability disputes.
6.3(1) *Defined.* *"Negotiability dispute"* is a dispute arising in good faith during the course of collective bargaining as to whether a proposal is subject to collective bargaining under the Act.
6.3(2) *Expedited resolution.* In the event that a negotiability dispute arises between the employer and the certified employee organization, either party may petition the board for expedited resolution of the dispute. The petition shall set forth the material facts of the dispute, the precise question of negotiability submitted for resolution, and certificate of service upon the other party. The parties shall present evidence on all issues to the fact finder or arbitrator, including the issue which is the subject of the negotiability dispute. A negotiability dispute raised at the fact-finding hearing shall be upon written objection to the submission of the proposal to the fact finder or arbitrator. The objection shall request the fact finder or arbitrator to seek a negotiability ruling from the board regarding the proposal or state that the objecting party will file a petition for resolution of the dispute with the board. In the event a negotiability dispute arises at the arbitration stage of impasse procedures, either party may petition the board for expedited resolution, which petition shall be filed within seven (7) days of the submission of final offers. Arbitrators and fact finders shall rule on all issues submitted to them including the issue which is the subject of the negotiability dispute unless explicitly stayed by the board. Arbitration awards and fact finder's recommendations issued prior to the final determination of the negotiability dispute will be contingent upon that determination.
6.3(3) *Decisions.* The petition filed pursuant to subrule 6.3(2) shall be given priority by the board. If deemed necessary by the board, the petition may be set for hearing or argument.

621—6.4(20) Acceptance of proposed agreement. Where the parties have reached a proposed (or "tentative") collective bargaining agreement, the terms of that agreement shall be made public, and the employee organization shall give reasonable notice of the date, time and place of a ratification election on the tentative agreement to the public employees; provided, however, that such notice shall be at least twenty-four (24) hours prior to the election and the election shall be within seven (7) days of the date of the tentative agreement. The vote shall be by secret ballot and only members of the employee organization shall be entitled to vote; provided, however, that the employee organization may, pursuant to its internal procedures, extend voting rights to nonmember bargaining unit employees. The employee organization shall within twenty-four (24) hours notify the public employer whether the proposed agreement has been ratified.
The public employer shall, within ten (10) days of the tentative agreement, likewise meet to accept or reject the agreement, and shall within twenty-four (24) hours serve notice on the employee organization of its acceptance or rejection of the proposed agreement; provided, however, that the public employer shall not be required to either accept or reject the tentative agreement if it has been rejected by the employee organization.
The above time limits may be modified by a written mutual agreement between the public employer and the employee organization.
The above time limits shall not apply to proposed agreements between the state and any bargaining unit of state employees.

621—6.5(20) Negotiations report—filing of agreement. Not later than sixty (60) days after conclusion of an agreement, the public employer shall submit to the board a report of negotiations procedures on a form provided by the board and shall attach two (2) copies of the agreement.

These rules are intended to implement Iowa Code chapter 20.

[Filed 3/4/75]

|Filed 10/29/76, Notice 9/22/76—published 11/17/76, effective 12/22/76|

|Filed 10/26/77, Notice 9/21/77—published 11/16/77, effective 12/21/77|

[Filed 2/3/78, Notice 12/28/77—published 2/22/78, effective 3/29/78]

[Filed 9/11/79, Notice 7/11/79—published 10/3/79, effective 11/12/79]

[Filed 11/7/80, Notice 9/17/80—published 11/26/80, effective 12/31/80]

[Filed 10/22/82, Notice 9/15/82—published 11/10/82, effective 12/15/82]

[Filed emergency 7/23/85—published 8/14/85, effective 7/23/85]

[Filed 10/9/86, Notice 8/27/86—published 11/5/86, effective 12/10/86]

CHAPTER 7
IMPASSE PROCEDURES

621—7.1(20) General. Except as provided in subrule 7.5(6), the rules set forth in this chapter are applicable only in the absence of an impasse agreement between the parties or the failure of either to utilize its procedures. Nothing in these rules shall be deemed to prohibit the parties, by mutual agreement, from proceeding directly to binding arbitration at any time after impasse.

621—7.2(20)* Fees of neutrals. Qualified fact finders, arbitrators and teacher termination adjudicators appointed from a list maintained by the board may be compensated by a sum not to exceed three hundred dollars ($300) per day of service, plus their necessary expenses incurred.

621—7.3(20) Mediation.

7.3(1) *Request for mediation.* Either party in an impasse may request the board in writing to appoint a mediator to an impasse.

An original and one copy of the request for mediation shall be filed with the board and shall, in addition to the request for mediation, contain:

a. The name, address, business and resident telephone numbers of the requesting party, and its bargaining representative or chairperson of the bargaining team of the requesting party.

b. The name, address, business and resident telephone numbers of the opposing party to the impasse, and its bargaining representative or chairperson of the bargaining team.

c. A description of the collective bargaining unit or units involved and the approximate number of employees in each unit.

d. A concise and specific listing of the negotiated items upon which the parties have reached impasse.

7.3(2) *Date, signature and notice.* The request for mediation shall be dated and signed by the requesting party. The requesting party shall also serve a copy of the request upon other parties to the negotiations either by personal delivery or by ordinary mail.

---

*Effective date of 12/15/82 delayed by the administrative rules review committee forty-five days after convening of the next General Assembly pursuant to § 17A.8(9).

7.3(3) *Appointment of mediator.* Upon receipt of a request for mediation, the board may appoint an impartial and disinterested person as mediator of the dispute and notify all parties of the appointment of the mediator. The board shall determine the effective date of this appointment.

7.3(4) *Confidential nature of mediation.* Any information, either written or oral, disclosed by the parties to the mediator in the performance of mediation duties shall not be discussed by the mediator voluntarily or by compulsion unless approved by the parties involved.

The mediator shall not disclose any information with regard to any mediation conducted on behalf of any party to any cause pending in a proceeding before a court, board, investigatory body, arbitrator or fact finder without the written consent of the public employment relations board. Without such written consent, the mediator shall respectfully decline, by reason of this rule, to divulge any information disclosed by a party in the performance of the mediator's duties.

7.3(5) *Mediation proceedings.* The mediator may hold separate or joint meetings with the parties or their representatives, and those meetings shall not be public. Mediation meetings shall be conducted at a time and place designated by the mediator. If an impasse exists ten (10) days after the effective date of the appointment of a mediator, the mediator shall so notify the board.

7.3(6) *Board mediator.* When the mediator is an employee of the Public Employment Relations Board, that mediator shall not participate in any contested case arising out of any transaction or occurrence relating to those mediation activities.

7.3(7) *Costs of mediation.* The mediator shall submit in writing to the board a list of fees and expenses.

621—7.4(20) Fact-finding.

7.4(1) *Appointment of fact finder.* Upon notification by the mediator that the dispute remains unresolved, or if the dispute remains unsolved ten (10) days after the appointment of the mediator, the board shall appoint a fact finder. Where the parties and the mediator agree, the board shall appoint the mediator to serve as fact finder. The board may permit the parties to select their fact finder from a list of qualified neutrals maintained by the board. The board retains the authority to appoint a fact finder as provided in Iowa Code section 20.21.

7.4(2) *Powers of the fact finder.* The fact finder shall have the power to conduct a hearing, administer oaths and request the board to issue subpoenas. The subject of fact-finding shall be the impasse items unresolved by mediation. By mutual agreement, the fact finder may also assist the parties in negotiating a settlement.

7.4(3) *Notice of hearing and exchange of proposal.* The appointment of the fact finder shall be effective the date of the commencement of the fact-finding hearing. The board or fact finder shall establish the time, place and date of hearing and shall notify the parties of the same. The parties shall exchange copies of all proposals to be presented to the fact finder at least five (5) days prior to the commencement of the fact-finding hearing; provided, however, that the parties may continue to bargain and nothing in this section shall preclude a party from making a concession or amending its proposals in the course of further bargaining. No party shall present a proposal to the fact finder which has not been offered to the other party in the course of negotiations.

7.4(4) *Briefs and statements.* The fact finder may require the parties to submit a brief or a statement on the unresolved impasse items.

7.4(5) *Hearing.* A fact-finding hearing shall be open to the public and shall be limited to matters which will enable the fact finder to make recommendations for settlement of the dispute.

7.4(6) *Report of the fact finder.* Within fifteen (15) days of appointment, the fact finder shall issue to the parties a "Report of Fact Finder" consisting of specific findings of fact concerning each impasse item, and separate therefrom, specific recommendations for resolution of each impasse item. In addition, the report shall recite the impasse items resolved by the parties during fact-finding and withdrawn from further impasse procedures. The report shall also identify the parties and their representatives and recite the time, date, place and duration of hearing sessions. The fact finder shall serve a copy of the report to the parties and file the original with the board.

7.4(7) *Action on fact finder's report.* Upon receipt of the fact finder's report, the public employer and the certified employee organization shall immediately accept the fact finder's recommendations or shall within five (5) days submit the fact finder's recommendations to the governing body and members of the certified employee organization for acceptance or rejection. "Immediately" shall mean a period of not longer than seventy-two (72) hours from said receipt. Notice to members of the employee organization shall be as provided in 6.4(20).

7.4(8) *Publication of report by board.* If the public employer and the employee organization fail to conclude a collective bargaining agreement ten (10) days after their receipt of the fact finder's report and recommendations, the board shall make the fact finder's report and recommendations available to the public.

7.4(9) *Cost of fact-finding.* The fact finder shall submit to the parties a written statement of fee and expenses with a copy sent to the board. The parties shall share the costs of fact-finding equally.

621—7.5(20) Binding arbitration.

7.5(1) *Request for arbitration.* At any time following the making public by the board of the fact finder's report and recommendations, either party to an impasse may request the board to initiate binding arbitration.

7.5(2) *Form and contents of request.* The request for arbitration shall be in writing and shall include the name, address and signature of the requesting party and the capacity in which acting.

7.5(3) *Service of request.* The requesting party shall serve a copy of the request for arbitration upon the opposing party by ordinary mail.

7.5(4) *Preliminary information.* Within four (4) days of the filing of the request with the board for arbitration, each party shall submit to the board the following information:

a. Final offers shall not be amended. A party shall not submit an offer for arbitration which has not been offered to the other party in the course of negotiations.

b. Two (2) copies of the final offer of the party on each impasse item.

c. Two (2) copies of the agreed upon provisions of the proposed collective bargaining agreement.

d. The name of the parties' selected arbitrator, or name of a single arbitrator where the parties agree to submit the dispute to a single arbitrator.

e. Certificate of service upon the opposing party of items *"b"* and *"d"* above.

7.5(5) *Selection of chairperson.* Within eight (8) days of the filing of the request for arbitration, the arbitrators selected by each party shall attempt to agree upon the selection of a third person to act as chairperson of the arbitration panel. If the parties to the impasse fail to agree upon an arbitration chairperson within the time allotted under this rule, the board shall submit a list of three (3) persons who have agreed to act as arbitration chairperson to the parties. The parties shall then select the arbitration chairperson from the list as provided by the Act.

7.5(6) *Conduct of hearings.* Arbitration hearings shall be open to the public, and shall be recorded either by mechanized means or by a certified shorthand reporter. The arbitration hearing shall be limited to those factors listed in Iowa Code section 20.22 and such other relevant factors as may enable the arbitrator or arbitration panel to select the fact finder's recommendation or the final offer of either party for each impasse item. Arbitrators appointed pursuant to impasse procedures agreed upon by the parties shall likewise consider the factors listed in section 20.22.

7.5(7) *Continued bargaining.* The parties may continue to bargain on the impasse items before the arbitrator or arbitration panel until the arbitrator or arbitration panel announces its decision. Should the parties reach agreement on an impasse item, they shall immediately report their agreement to the arbitrator or arbitration panel. The arbitrator or arbitration panel shall add the agreed upon term to the collective bargaining contract and shall no longer consider the final offers of the parties or the fact finder's recommendation on that impasse item.

7.5(8) *Report of the arbitrator or arbitration panel.* Within fifteen (15) days after its first meeting (unless such time period is waived by the parties), the arbitrator or arbitration panel shall issue the award and serve each party and the board with a copy by ordinary mail. In reaching the panel decision, the chairperson may communicate telephonically, by mail, or may meet individually or collectively with the other panel members.

7.5(9) *Dismissal of arbitrator or arbitration panel.* In the event of a failure of the arbitrator or arbitration panel to issue the award within fifteen (15) days of the first meeting, the arbitrator or chairperson of the arbitration panel shall notify the board and the parties of this failure. Either party may thereafter request a new arbitrator or arbitration panel. Unless the parties agree otherwise, the procedures in subrules 7.5(1) to 7.5(5) shall apply; provided, however, that the parties may submit new final offers and nominate different arbitrators. No arbitrator or arbitration panel shall issue a partial award except by mutual consent of the parties.

7.5(10) *Costs of arbitration.* The arbitrator shall submit to the parties a written statement of fees and expenses with a copy sent to the board. The parties shall share the costs of arbitration equally.

621—7.6(20) Impasse procedures after budget certification.

7.6(1) *Objections.* Any objection by a party to the conduct of fact-finding proceedings which will not be completed by the budget certification date, or arbitration proceedings which will not be completed by the budget certification date, shall be filed with the board and served upon the other party no later than ten (10) days after receipt of a request for fact-finding or arbitration, or twenty (20) days prior to the budget certification date, whichever occurs later. Failure to file an objection in a timely manner may constitute waiver of such objection, in which case the budget certification deadline for completion of impasse procedures shall not apply.

7.6(2) *Response to objection.* The party which requested fact-finding or arbitration may within ten (10) days file a response to the objection, asserting that, because of deliberate delay on the part of the objecting party, or unavoidable casualty, misfortune or other events beyond the parties' control, impasse procedures should continue beyond the budget certification deadline. If response is not filed within ten (10) days of receipt of the objection, the board may issue an order terminating further impasse procedures.

7.6(3) *Procedure.* Filing of an objection before the budget certification date shall not affect the obligation of each party to continue the impasse procedures. Further, the board may postpone hearing on the objection if it determines that a fact finder's recommendation or arbitration award may be rendered on or before the budget certification date; in making that determination, the board will attempt to expedite any remaining impasse proceedings, but no party shall be required to waive or shorten any mandatory statutory time periods which apply to that party.

7.6(4) *Hearings.* Insofar as is applicable, hearings shall be conducted pursuant to chapter 2 of these rules. The party seeking fact-finding or arbitration shall proceed first and shall have the burden to show that fact-finding or arbitration should not be terminated. The board shall then issue a final order, finding that further impasse procedures should be either terminated or completed.

621—7.7(20) Impasse procedures for state employees.
7.7(1) *Procedures.* Statutory procedures in Iowa Code sections 20.20 to 20.22, and independent impasse procedures negotiated by the parties must provide that the impasse be submitted to binding arbitration and the arbitration hearing concluded no later than February 28, and that any arbitrator's award will be issued on or before March 15. This rule does not preclude the parties from mutually agreeing to a date other than February 28, but the agreement must result in an arbitration award on or before March 15.

7.7(2) *Independent procedures.* Independent impasse procedures negotiated by the parties must provide that the impasse will be submitted to binding arbitration, and any hearing thereon concluded no later than February 28, and that any arbitrator's award will be issued on or before March 15.

7.7(3) *Statutory procedures.* In the absence of independent procedures, the procedures in sections 20.20 to 20.22 and rules 7.1(20) to 7.5(20) shall apply, except that a single party request for mediation must be filed no later than December 14 and the appointment of a fact finder by the board will be made by December 24, effective the date of hearing, which shall be no later than January 10. A request for binding arbitration must be filed by February 1, and any impasse must be submitted to the arbitrator(s), and hearing concluded no later than February 28.

7.7(4) *New certifications.* Statutory impasse procedures under these rules shall not be available if the employee organization has been certified later than December 1. This rule does not preclude the parties from negotiating independent impasse procedures if an employee organization is certified after December 1 and the procedures will result in an arbitration award on or before March 15.

7.7(5) *Negotiability disputes.* Disputes concerning the negotiability of any subject of bargaining shall be submitted to the board for determination pursuant to subrule 6.3(20) no later than March 1. An arbitration award rendered prior to final determination of the negotiability dispute will be made conditional upon such determination. Notwithstanding the provisions of subrule 2.19(20) no stay of impasse procedures will be granted during the pendency of any negotiability dispute, declaratory ruling request, or prohibited practice complaint.

This rule is intended to implement Iowa Code section 20.17.

These rules are intended to implement Iowa Code chapter 20.

[Filed 3/4/75]
[Filed Emergency 12/30/75—published 1/26/76, effective 12/30/75]
[Filed 10/29/76, Notice 9/22/76—published 11/17/76, effective 12/22/76]
[Filed Emergency 10/26/77 after Notice 9/21/77—published 11/16/77, effective 11/1/77]
[Filed 10/26/77, Notice 9/21/77—published 11/16/77, effective 12/21/77]
[Filed 9/11/79, Notice 7/11/79—published 10/3/79, effective 11/12/79]
[Filed 11/7/80, Notice 9/17/80—published 11/26/80, effective 12/31/80]
[Filed 10/22/82, Notice 9/15/82—published 11/10/82, effective 12/15/82*]
[Filed emergency 7/23/85—published 8/14/85, effective 7/23/85]
[Filed 10/9/86, Notice 8/27/86—published 11/5/86, effective 12/10/86]

---

*Effective date of 7.2 delayed by the administrative rules review committee forty-five days after convening of the next General Assembly pursuant to § 17A.8(9).

CHAPTER 8
INTERNAL CONDUCT OF EMPLOYEE ORGANIZATIONS

621—8.1(20) Registration report.
8.1(1) *When filed.* Before an employee organization may be certified as the exclusive representative of a bargaining unit, the employee organization shall have filed a registration report with the board.
8.1(2) *Form and content.* The registration report shall be in a form prescribed by the board. The registration report shall be accompanied by two (2) copies of the employee organization's constitution and bylaws. A filing by a national or international of its constitution and bylaws shall be accepted in lieu of a filing of such documents by each subordinate organization, provided that such national or international constitution and bylaws conform to the requirements of the Act.

621—8.2(20) Annual report.
8.2(1) *When filed.* Before an employee organization may be certified as the exclusive representative of a bargaining unit, the employee organization shall have filed an annual report with the board. Such reports shall be filed within ninety (90) days of the conclusion of each fiscal year of the employee organization. The first annual report filed by an employee organization may be filed concurrently with an election petition and shall reflect the last completed fiscal year of the organization or, in the case of a new organization, the last completed quarter or quarters of the current fiscal year.
8.2(2) *Form and content.* The annual report shall be in a form prescribed by the board and shall contain:
  a. The names and addresses of the organization, any parent organization or organizations with which it is affiliated, the principal officers and all representatives.
  b. The name and address of its local agent for service of process.
  c. A general description of the public employees the organization represents or seeks to represent.
  d. The amounts of the initiation fee and monthly dues members must pay.
  e. A pledge, in a form prescribed by the board, that the organization will comply with the laws of the state and that it will accept members without regard to age, race, sex, religion, national origin or physical disability, as provided by law.
  f. A financial report and audit. The financial report shall contain, at a minimum, the following information: Cash balance from the previous year; a listing of sources and amounts of income; an identified listing of disbursements; and a closing balance. The audit should be separate from the financial report and consist of a statement that the financial report has been reviewed and found to be true and accurate. The audit must be signed by a person or persons who hold no other office in the employee organization and who did not prepare the financial report.

621—8.3(20) Bonding requirements. Every person required by section 20.25(3)*"c"* of the Code to be bonded shall be bonded to provide protection against loss by reason of act of fraud or dishonesty on the part of such person, directly or through connivance with others. The bond of each such person shall be fixed at the beginning of the employees organization's fiscal year and shall be in an amount of not less then ten percent (10%) of the funds handled by such person or their predecessor or predecessors, if any, during the preceding fiscal year, but in no case less than two thousand dollars ($2,000) nor more than five hundred thousand dollars ($500,000). If the employee organization or the trust in which an employee organization is interested does not have a preceding fiscal year, the amount of the bond shall not be less than two thousand dollars ($2,000). Such bonds shall have a corporate surety company as surety thereon. Any person who is not covered by such bonds shall not be permitted to receive, handle, disburse or otherwise exercise control of the funds or other property of an employee organization or of a trust in which an employee organization is interested. No such bond shall be placed through an agent or broker or with a surety company in which any employee organization or any officer, agent, shop steward or other representative of an employee organization has any direct or indirect interest.

621—8.4(20) Trusteeships.

8.4(1) *Establishment.* Trusteeships shall be established or administered by an organization over a subordinate employee organization only in accordance with the constitution and bylaws of the organization which has assumed trusteeship over the subordinate body and for the purpose of correcting corruption or financial malpractice, assuring the performance of collective bargaining agreements or other duties of a bargaining representative, restoring democratic procedures or otherwise carrying out the legitimate objectives of the employee organization.

8.4(2) *Reports.* Every organization which assumes trusteeship over any subordinate employee organization shall file with the board within thirty (30) days after the imposition of any such trusteeship, and semiannually thereafter, a report, signed by its president and treasurer or corresponding principal officers, as well as by the trustees of such subordinate employee organization, containing the following information:

  a. The name and address of the subordinate employee organization;
  b. The date of the establishment of the trusteeship;
  c. A detailed statement of the reason for the establishment or the continuation of the trusteeship; and
  d. The nature and extent of participation by the membership of the subordinate employee organization in the selection of delegates to represent such employee organization in regular or special conventions or other policy-determining bodies and in the election of officers of the organization which has assumed trusteeship over the employee organization.

  The initial report of the establishment of the trusteeship shall include a full and complete account of the financial condition of the subordinate employee organization as of the time trusteeship was assumed over it.

8.4(3) *Continuing duty to report.* During the continuance of a trusteeship, the organization which has assumed trusteeship over a subordinate employee organization shall file on behalf of the subordinate employee organization all reports required by this chapter. Such reports shall be signed by the president and treasurer or corresponding principal officers of the organization which has assumed such trusteeship and the trustees of the subordinate employee organization.

621—8.5(20) Reports as public information.

8.5(1) *Use by the board.* The contents of the reports required by this chapter shall be public information, and the board may publish any information and data which it obtains from such reports.

8.5(2) *Available to the public.* The board shall make reasonable provisions for inspection and examination, at the request of any person, of any report required to be filed with the board by this chapter.

621—8.6(20) Filing of a complaint.

A complaint that any employee organization has engaged in or is engaging in any practice which constitutes a violation of Iowa Code section 20.25 may be filed in writing with the board by any affected person. Upon receipt of a complaint, the board shall serve a copy upon the employee organization by certified mail, return receipt requested. The board shall conduct a preliminary investigation of the alleged violation. In conducting the investigation, the board may require the production of evidence, including affidavits and documents. If investigation shows the complaint has no basis in fact, the complaint shall be dismissed and the parties notified. If the investigation shows reasonable cause to believe a violation has occurred, the board shall notify the parties. If the parties are unable to agree on an informal settlement after notification of reasonable cause, the board shall schedule the complaint for hearing.

These rules are intended to implement Iowa Code chapter 20.

[Filed 3/4/75]

[Filed 10/29/76, Notice 9/22/76—published 11/17/76, effective 12/22/76]

[Filed 11/7/80, Notice 9/17/80—published 11/26/80, effective 12/31/81]

[Filed 10/9/86, Notice 8/27/86—published 11/5/86, effective 12/10/86]

CHAPTER 9
ADMINISTRATIVE REMEDIES

621—9.1(20) Final decisions. A cross-appeal may be taken within the 20 days for taking an appeal or within five days after the appeal is taken. When a quorum of the members of the board presides at initial hearing on any matter, the decision entered thereon is a final decision of the agency. When the hearing is presided over by other than a quorum of the members of the board, the administrative law judge shall render a proposed decision, which shall become the final decision of the agency unless within 20 days of the filing of such decision:

    9.1(1)   A party aggrieved by the decision files a written notice of appeal with the board, or

    9.1(2)   The board, on its own motion, determines to review the decision.

621—9.2(20) Appeals to board.

    9.2(1) *Grounds for appeal.* Any proposed decision of an administrative law judge may be modified, reversed or set aside by the board on one or more of the following grounds:

    a. That the administrative law judge acted without or in excess of the administrative law judge's powers;

    b. That the proposed decision was procured by fraud or is contrary to law;

    c. That the facts found by the administrative law judge do not support the proposed decision;

    d. That the proposed decision is not supported by a preponderance of the competent evidence on the record considered as a whole;

    e. That the conduct of the hearing or any ruling made therein has resulted in prejudicial error;

    f. That a substantial question of law or policy is raised because of the absence of or departure from officially reported board precedent;

    g. That there are compelling reasons for reconsideration of an important board rule or policy.

    9.2(2) *Notice of appeal.* The notice of appeal shall be in writing, addressed to the board, and shall set forth the specific grounds for appeal. The appealing party shall deliver a copy to opposing parties by ordinary mail.

    9.2(3) *Hearing.* The board may hear the case de novo or upon the record as submitted before the administrative law judge. Any person, employee organization or public employer who has a significant interest in the outcome of the appeal may petition the board for intervention in the appeal proceedings. Where intervention is granted by the board, the intervening parties may submit briefs and arguments and participate in the same manner as an original party to the proceeding. The board shall set a time and place of hearing or argument and give notice thereof to the parties. The decision rendered by the board shall be a final decision of the agency.

    9.3(20)   Rescinded, effective December 21, 1977.

These rules are intended to impement Iowa Code chapter 20.

[Filed 3/4/75]

|Filed 10/26/77, Notice 9/21/77—published 11/16/77, effective 12/21/77|

[Filed 9/11/79, Notice 7/11/79—published 10/3/79, effective 11/12/79]

[Filed 11/7/80, Notice 9/17/80—published 11/26/80, effective 12/31/80]

[Filed eme: gency 7/23/85—published 8/14/85, effective 7/23/85]

[Filed 10/9/86, Notice 8/27/86—published 11/5/86, effective 12/10/86]

[Filed 2/1/89, Notice 12/28/88—published 2/22/89, effective 3/30/89]

CHAPTER 10
DECLARATORY RULINGS

621—10.1(17A,20) Who may petition. Any person, public employer or employee organization may petition the board to issue a declaratory ruling as to the applicability of any statutory provision, rule or other written statement of law or policy, decision or order of the agency.

621—10.2(20) Contents of petition. A petition for declaratory ruling shall include:
10.2(1) The name, address and phone number of the petitioner.
10.2(2) The specific facts upon which the board is to base its declaratory ruling upon the questions presented.
10.2(3) The specific questions upon which the petitioner seeks a declaratory ruling.
10.2(4) Certificate of service upon any other parties directly involved in the matter.

621—10.3(17A,20) Clarifications. The board may require the petitioner to clarify either the facts or questions presented by the petition.

621—10.4(17A,20) Caption. The following caption is suggested for petitions for declaratory rulings:

BEFORE THE PUBLIC EMPLOYMENT RELATIONS BOARD

IN THE MATTER OF:		CASE NO.
[NAME OF THE PARTY REQUESTING THE RULING] PETITIONER	}	PETITION FOR DECLARATORY RULING

621—10.5(17A,20) Service. If a petition for declaratory ruling is based upon specific facts or raises specific questions which directly involve another party, that party shall be served with a copy of the petition by ordinary mail.

621—10.6(17A,20) Intervention. See rule 2.4(20).
These rules are intended to implement Iowa Code sections 17A.9 and chapter 20.
[Filed 10/29/76, Notice 9/22/76—published 11/17/76, effective 12/22/76]
[Filed 11/7/80, Notice 9/17/80—published 11/26/80, effective 12/31/80]
[Filed 10/9/86, Notice 8/27/86—published 11/5/86, effective 12/10/86]

Annotated Bibliography

Blackwood, Toni. "Illegal Public Employee Strikes: Allowing a Civil Suit for Damages." *University of Missouri Kansas City Law Review* 53, no. 2 (Winter 1985): 299–310.
The Missouri Public Sector Labor Law governing public employee labor relations does not provide sanctions for strikes. The Kansas City Firefighters court case greatly expands Missouri law by implying the right to bring civil action under a statute that does not provide for such action. This court case raises the question of what impact such action will have on public employee unions, its members, and private citizens. Legislature should provide a more certain framework designed to provide an equitable distribution of power among both parties.

Chairman, Practicing Law Institute. *Public Sector Labor Relations, Litigation and Administrative Practice Series, Litigation, Course Handbook Series*, nos. 126, 159, and 201; and *Corporate Law and Practice, Course Handbook Series*, no. 84. Practicing Law Institute, New York, N.Y., 1978, 1980, 1982.
Course handbooks prepared to serve as educational supplements and reference manuals to program participants, attorneys, and related professionals unable to attend program sessions. Each program begins with an overview of recent developments in public sector labor relations and law and continues into specific areas of interest as presented in the

papers subsequently published. The individual presenters and authors include attorneys, administrators, and arbitrators in the field of public sector labor relations.

D.P.H. "California Public Employees Granted Right to Strike Without Legislative Authority." *Washington University Law Quarterly* 64 (Spring 1986): 263–270.

Traditionally, public employees have been refused the right to strike against their employers under common law. Several states, including California, have enacted statutory exceptions that allow public employee strikes under certain exceptions; the specificity of the states' legislation varies. The author feels that the legislature is the best place for policy determination for definition of terms and labor resolution procedures; the court decision in County Sanitation fails to recognize judicial limitations in its policy analysis and should entice legislative clarification.

Fain, Gregory Thomas. "Local Public Employees Right to Strike After County Sanitation District v. Los Angeles County Employees Association." *Pacific Law Journal* 17 (January 1986): 533–552.

In 1985, the California Supreme Court recognized the right of public employees to strike, provided they do not affect "essential services." This comment analyzes California law prior to the County Sanitation case and compares the right to strike in the public and private sectors. The author further reviews the statutes of other states for consideration by the California legislature in developing a statute that will benefit both public employee unions and management by providing mandatory special impasse procedures.

Gilbert, Gay M. "Dispute Resolution Techniques and Public Sector Collective Bargaining." *Ohio State Journal on Dispute Resolution*, 2, no. 2 (Spring 1987): 287–309.

The article provides an overview of the primary techniques utilized by states in dispute resolution, explores variations in the methods used and the extrinsic factors that influence the method selected, and evaluates how the variation selected impacts the utility and effectiveness of the techniques. A review of the Ohio Collective Bargaining Law for Public Employees provides an example of the impact on a dispute resolution technique caused by legislative configuration and structure. Due to the relatively new nature of public sector collective bargaining and the unique problems that arise in the public sector, states will continue to experiment and develop technique variation and configuration.

Gill, Timothy M. "Public Employee Strikes: Legalization Through the Elimination of Remedies." *California Law Review* 72 (July 1984): 629–660.

The 1983 California Supreme Court decisions in two important cases bearing on the right of public employees to strike have made strikes a more feasible bargaining tactic for employees, unless specifically prohibited by statute. Public employee strikes are no longer illegal in California under either collective bargaining statutes or the rationale of common law. Although the court has formulated a case-by-case analytical approach based on public employers' remedies, further development of consistent and rational case law will be needed to guide lower courts in resolving the tremendous range of issues and variety of strike situations that arise.

Goetz, Raymond. "The Kansas Public Employer–Employee Relations Law." *Kansas Law Review* 28 (Winter 1980): 243–289.

This article analyzes the 1971 Kansas Public Employer–Employee Relations Act, a meet and confer bill necessarily vague as to the manner and scope with which parties conduct negotiations. The act covers state employees, exclusive of teachers, with municipal coverage optional. Experience has demonstrated no serious problems with administrative procedure; it remains to be seen how long and well the act's procedures will withstand public employee demands against employer resistance.

Grant, Jack. "A Primer of Unit Design Under Ohio's Public Employees' Collective Bargaining Statute." *University of Dayton Law Review* 11, no. 2 (Winter 1986): 221–239.

This article focuses discussion on the third element required under Ohio's collective bargaining statute before bargaining can begin: the appropriate unit designation. The unit fixes the components of the voting constituency that will decide its exclusive representative and its appropriateness for representation. Unit design has seven conditioning dependencies, which can be manipulated to achieve appropriate legal and efficient units.

Grodin, Joseph R., Wollett, Donald H., and Alleyene, Reginald H., Jr. *Collective Bargaining in Public Employment.* 3d ed. *Unit*

Four of Labor Relations and Social Problems, a Course Book.
Washington, D.C.: The Bureau of National Affairs, Inc., 1979.
   This course book has been developed by the Labor Law Group,
originally organized in 1971 by a group of law teachers interested
in teaching students in labor relations in a nontraditional format and
concerned with the context of law school teaching materials. It attempts
to present materials to identify policy issues implicit to public sector
labor relations law and to illustrate the arguments and solutions brought
before legislatures, courts, and administrative agencies. This approach
is of value to the lawyer as policy formulator and advocate.

Haviland, John F., Jr. and Hunt, Colleen M. "S.133: Ohio's Public-
   Sector Collective-Bargaining Framework." *University of Dayton
   Law Review* 9 (Summer 1984): 583–606.
   The Ohio general assembly has provided a comprehensive statutory framework controlling all aspects of public employment relations
with the passage of S.133. This note provides a historical perspective
of the factors and decisions that prompted passage of this bill and
an analysis of the right to strike and binding arbitration provisions.
These provisions could lead to improved public relations problems
and a stabilized public sector work force, which would enable local
governments to provide essential services more effectively.

Helsby, Robert D., Harral, William B., and Shane, Joseph. *Three
   Neighboring States—Three Different Approaches to Labor Relations.* Washington, D.C.: Labor Management Relation Service
   of the National League of Cities, U.S. Conference of Mayors,
   National Association of Counties, 1973.
   A special report detailing the different approaches and experience of three adjoining states in dealing with the unionization of
public employees. The individual reports were prepared by persons
participating at a responsible level of labor relations in the respective
states. The consulting reports were issued for assistance and use by
states, counties, and cities contemplating new or amended collective
bargaining legislation.

Hunter, Michael. "Public Employee Collective Bargaining Becomes A
   Matter of Right In Ohio." *Capital University Law Review* 13
   (Winter 1983): 219–252.

The author provides a history of legal developments in Ohio leading to employee collective bargaining law and its similarities to and differences with the National Labor Relations Act. Focus is directed on the scope of bargaining under the act and the determination of appropriate bargaining units. The author provides suggestions for implementation of the law, with particular emphasis in these focal areas.

Kochan, Thomas A., editor. *Challenges and Choices Facing American Labor*. Cambridge, Mass.: MIT Press, 1985.
This book is a collection of papers prepared by labor economists and industrial relations scholars under a three-year study of U.S. industrial relations in transition sponsored by the Sloan Foundation. The authors' contributions represent an up-to-date summary of the causes of the upheaval in industrial relations. Included in the collection are discussions on challenges to union organizing, labor market and technological developments, developments in collective bargaining, and unions and quality-of-work-life programs.

Leibig, Michael T. and Kahn, Wendy L. *Public Employee Organizing and the Law*. Washington, D.C.: The Bureau of National Affairs, Inc., 1987.
This book provides a basic guide to the rules of organizing state and local employees in the academic training setting and in the practical organizing campaign. It is concerned with law and how it works in public sector union organizing. An overview is given of organizing drive issues, state-by-state statutes, organizing rules, analysis of state and local collective bargaining structures, and resource materials for use by organizers.

Leonard, Arthur S. "Collective Bargaining on Issues of Health and Safety in the Public Sector: The Experience Under New York's Taylor Law." *Buffalo Law Review* 31(Winter 1982): 165–190.
The Public Employment Relations Board (PERB), the agency charged with administration of the New York Public Employees Fair Employment Act, has frequently been confronted with bargaining demands by public sector unions in New York for determination whether a particular health and safety issue comes within the scope of the statutory negotiating duty. PERB has restricted the scope of negotiations by

holding that particular demands relating directly to the manner and means of providing service to the public constitute policy making and are not directly subject to the bargaining process, while other approaches regarding these same demands have been presented as terms and conditions of employment and, thus, subject to bargaining. Careful articulation of decision theory and avoidance of past inconsistencies by PERB will provide guidance to public employers faced with new statutory duties in the field of employee health and safety.

Levine, Marvin J. *Comparative Labor Relations Law*. Morristown, N.J.: General Learning Press, 1975.
A casebook approach to analysis of the legal aspects of public sector labor relations to be used by students, government administrators, officials of public employee unions, practitioners, and laymen. The chapters cover areas at the federal, state, and local levels of public employment. Similarities and differences between public and private sector labor relations are emphasized by comparing administrative rulings and court decisions with NLRB determinations.

McGuire, Melissa M. "The Effect of New York's Triborough Law on Public Sector Labor Negotiations." *Albany Law Review* 48 (Winter 1984): 459–493.
The Triborough Doctrine, developed by New York's PERB, was developed to preserve the status quo during negotiations when one contract expired without agreement on its successor. It led to legislation known as the Triborough Law, which gives employees unprecedented security during the interim between contracts. The note explores the manner and reasons for development of the Triborough Doctrine and its subsequent codification. As a result, the Triborough Law may negatively complicate and prolong negotiations between public employers and their employees.

Mills, Miriam K., editor. *Alternative Dispute Resolution in the Public Sector*. Chicago: Nelson-Hall Publishers, 1991.
A symposium that presents considerations on conflict resolution approaches to labor relations, environmental issues, rule making, and related conflicts, which include adjudication by third parties and joint decision making by the disputing parties. Alternative Dispute Resolution (ADR), the resolution of disputes by means other than

litigation, is analyzed within a number of settings; policy implications of various models are assessed. In the editor's view, ADR may be the best approach to conclusively reaching settlements.

Norwood, Ronald Alan. "Prima Facie Tort—A Judicial Reaction to Public Employee Strikes in Missouri." *Missouri Law Review* 50 (Summer 1985): 687–703.

While other jurisdictions have allowed civil redress for illegal public employee strikes, Missouri has become the first jurisdiction to allow a party injured by an illegal strike to recover under prima facie tort theory. This note analyzes the Missouri court case decision and considers whether civil remedies, more specifically, prima facie tort findings, are appropriate for public employee strikes. The use of such remedies can serve to protect vital public services and deter public employee strikes; however, more-comprehensive legislation is needed for clarity in public service labor relations.

Ohio Department of Administrative Service. *Ohio Public Employer's Employee Relations Manual.* State of Ohio, 1974.

This publication was prepared through a grant from the U.S. Civil Service Commission under the Intergovernmental Personnel Act (IPA), an assistance program for all public officials seeking to improve public employee personnel systems. The manual discusses collective bargaining and its process, the legal environment for Ohio public sector employee relations, and contract administration and grievance procedures. The intent of the manual is to provide public officials with materials for positive guidance in developing policies and practices in dealing with employee relations.

O'Reilly, James T. "Ohio Strikes Back: Constitutional Invalidation of Labor Settlement Procedures." *University of Cincinnati Law Review* 57 (1989): 1351–1370.

In 1988, Ohio municipalities won a powerful court decision for city managers and city councils against union employees when the Ohio Supreme Court struck down the state's 1983 collective bargaining contract terms for the power to strike. The court decision opens other Ohio agencies and programs to challenges of violations and legislative authority. New challenges may severely effect other public programs, which may have more impact on the public than wage rates or employment conditions of civil servants.

Platt, Robert H. "Comparison of Impasse Procedures: The New York City Collective Bargaining Law and The New York State Taylor Law." *Fordham Urban Law Journal* 9 (1980–1981): 1039–1057.
New York State provides for collective bargaining for all public employees under the 1967 Taylor Law, but also permits any public employer to enact different provisions and procedures provided they are substantially equivalent for the regulation of employees. This note provides a review and comparison of the multitiered procedures provided for in the Taylor Law and the New York City Collective Bargaining Law (NYCCBL), covering the municipal agencies in New York City. The statistics for the period studied indicate strikes were more prevalent under the Taylor Law, which is indicative of the differing dispute resolution techniques utilized and the need for change to the Taylor Law.

Rehaut, Steven M. "California's SEERA vs. The Civil Service System: Making State Employee Collective Bargaining Work." *University of California, Davis, Law Review* 18 (Spring 1985): 829–864.
This comment highlights the nature of the conflict between the California Personnel Board and civil service system and the state employees' collective bargaining rights legislated under the 1977 State Employer–Employee Relations Act (SEERA). It further examines SEERA and the California Constitution to determine the extent to which employees should be allowed to negotiate on issues previously administered by the personnel board. The author concludes that the state has narrowed the scope of bargaining for state employees through misinterpretation of the constitution and should amend SEERA to clarify the civil service subjects of bargaining.

Rubin, Richard S., Hickman, Charles W., Durkee, William A., and Hayford, Stephen L. *Public Sector Unit Determination, Administrative Procedures and Case Law: A Comparative Evaluation of Executive Order 11491 and Selected State Collective Bargaining Frameworks. Final Report.* Bloomington: Midwest Center for Public Sector Labor Relations, Indiana University, School of Public and Environmental Affairs, May 31, 1978.
The report presents the results of a study undertaken for the Department of Labor on unit determination for the federal government.

The purposes of the study are to compile a comprehensive summary of procedures and criteria utilized by selected jurisdictions in creating bargaining units; to make a comparative examination of dominant trends in these jurisdictions and determine their impact on the stability of the bargaining relationship; and to develop policy and conclusions based on the data gathered and organized under the first two purposes. The results of the report could be used by interested parties and the public in deliberations over proposed legislative and regulations regarding public sector collective bargaining.

Shaw, Lori E. "Labor Law: The California Supreme Court Confers A Limited Right to Strike Upon California's Public Employees Through Judicial Fiat." *University of Dayton Law Review* 11 no. 2 (Winter 1986): 421–437.

The California Supreme Court became the only state court to deny the validity of the common law rule prohibiting strikes when statutory authority is absent. Although the court had the authority to modify the common law, public concern was not represented; this representation is best served in the legislature. Although the court provided a thorough analysis of the reasons for common law prohibition to public sector strikes, the California Supreme Court has set a precedent in labor law.

Wenkart, Ronald D. "Dismissal of California Public School Employees Engaged in Union Activity." *Santa Clara Law Review* 22 (Fall 1982): 1133–1149.

This article analyzes the "tests" adopted by the courts, the NLRB, and the California Public Employee Relations Board (PERB) to determine whether an employee has been discharged for lawful reasons and discusses how each test balances the competing interests of the employer and employee. The federal courts, the California Supreme Court, and the NLRB have adopted a narrow standard in the belief that labor relations legislation should not interfere with the employer's judgment or the efficient operation of enterprises. The PERB standard for determining whether employee union rights have been violated in discharge cases shifts the burden of proof to the public employer and hampers the ability of public sector employers to manage tax dollars efficiently. Efficient management of the public sector is demanded by today's taxpayers; therefore, the author argues that PERB should adopt the narrower standards applied by the courts and NLRB.

Werne, Benjamin. *The Law and Practice of Public Employment Labor Relations*, vols. 1–3. Charlottesville, Va.: The Michie Company, 1974.

This work, prepared by a U.S. Supreme Court member, focuses on the emerging law dealing with public sector collective bargaining at all levels. Volume 1 presents an overview of relevant factors and concepts related to the law and practices as well as sample clauses for contracts. Volume 2 deals with selected state statutes from various jurisdictions dealing with labor relations in the public sector. Volume 3 presents excerpts from orders, opinions, and other related matters issued at both the federal and state level.

White, Rebecca Hanner, Kaplan, Robert E., and Hawkins, Michael W. "Ohio's Public Employee Bargaining Law: Can it Withstand Constitutional Challenge?" *University of Cincinnati Law Review* 53, no. 1 (1984): 1–47.

This article analyzes the historical development of public employees' bargaining history and how constitutional questions have been handled by out-of-state courts. An overview of Ohio's 1983 Senate Bill 133 is provided, focusing on its provisions most likely to come under constitutional attack. It then examines out-of-state authority to provide a framework for resolving constitutional issues.

Wilson, Charles E. "The Replacement of Lawful Economic Strikes in the Public Sector in Ohio." *Ohio State Law Journal* 46 (1985): 639–687.

This article reviews the distinctions between private and public sector strikes, the legislative history of the Ohio Public Employees Collective Bargaining Law, due process clauses of Ohio, and the United States Constitution and the relevant precedents in other jurisdictions. Contrary to private sector principles, it is maintained that public employers should not have the right to replace permanently any public employees engaged in a lawful economic strike. The public employer's right to replace lawful strikers can be defined in a way to accommodate better the interests of both the public and government employers and employees.

Winograd, Barry. "San Jose Revisited: A Proposal for Negotiated Modification of Public Sector Bargaining Agreements Rejected Under Chapter 9 of the Bankruptcy Code." *Hastings Law Journal* 37 (November 1985): 231–333.

The article presents an analytical framework for reconciling federal bankruptcy law in relation to public and private sector labor relations. A proposal for reconciliation is made by the author that would bar unilateral action at the outset of any public sector bankruptcy. Renegotiation should be required before any modification of employment terms are allowed.

Index

Administrative law agency, 51; authority, 56; decision making, 54; enforcement role, 54–55; structure, 55–56

Alaniz v. City of San Antonio (Texas), 97

Alabama, 87

Alexander v. Gardner-Denver, 138

American Arbitration Association, 134

American Federation of Teachers, 65

American Federation of State County and Municipal Employees, 128

American Postal Workers Union, 132

Arbitration, 23; awards, 116, 136; ethics, arbitrators', 134; grievances, 129; outcomes, 119; suit for enforcement, 106

Baird, Charles W., 118

Bargaining unit, 23; determination, 68–70

Bell Aerospace, 69

Board of Supervisors v. NYPERB, 34

Bowen v. U.S. Postal Service, 132

Budgeting, 94, 142

Bureau of National Affairs, Inc., 24

California, 28–29, 59, 61, 87; Higher Education Bargaining Law, 29, 34, 56–58; impasse procedures, 103; Public Employment Relations Board, 58; San Francisco, 86

Checks and balances, 42
City of Detroit (Michigan
  MERC), 97
City of Saginaw (Michigan
  MERC),96
City of Sioux Falls v. Sioux Falls
  Firefighters, Local 814, 109
Civil Rights Act of 1871, 65
Civil Rights Act of 1964, 14, 93
Civil Service Reform Act of
  1978, 3–4, 83, 95
Collective bargaining, 3, 16–19,
  22, 28, 30–32, 51, 86–87; hard
  bargaining, 114; law as envi-
  ronment, 111; politics, 114; on
  principle, 113
Colorado, 86, 107
Commonwealth v. Pullis, 11
Concerted action, 66–67
Connecticut, 71–72; impasse
  procedures, 104
Criminal conspiracy, 8

Dade County v. Amalgamated
  Association of Street Electric
  Railway and Motor Coach
  Employees of America, 96
De facto bargaining, 31
DelCostello v. IBT, 133
Diseconomies, 46
Division 540, Amalgamated Tran-
  sit Union v. Mercer County
  Improvement Authority, 109
Dunlop, John T., 121–122

Efficiency, 42–43
Elections, 23
Employee rights, 24–25; fair
  representation, 131–134

Employer rights, 72–74
Externality, 38

Fact finding, 104–105, 114, 116
Fair Labor Standards Act, 14–15,
  93
Federal Mediation and Concili-
  ation Service, 105, 128, 134
Fellows v. La Tronica, 138
Friedman, Milton, 13

Gallagher, Daniel G., 116
General Shoe Corp., 70–71
Georgia, 87
Gissel Packing, NLRB v., 70
Globe Cotton Mills v. NLRB, 96
Good-faith, 75, 112–114; bar-
  gaining, 85–86, 88–92
Greeley Police Union v. City
  Council, 109
Guss v. Utah Labor Relations
  Board, 59

Hines v. Anchor Motor Freight,
  132
Hortonville Jt. School Dist. No.
  1 v. Hortonville Education
  Association, 79

Illinois, 33, 59; Cook County, 65
Impasse procedures, 29, 99; compulsory v. voluntary, 100–103;
  narcotic effect, 115
Income elasticity, 45
Indiana, 34, 52, 88, 102, 138;
  arbitration of grievances, 135;
  legislative action, pending,
  143; teacher unions, 117
Injunctions, 27

International Union of Operating Engineers, Local 321 v. Water Works Board of the City of Birmingham, 96
Iowa, 55, 72–73, 76–77, 79, 84–85, 88, 93, 96; arbitration of grievances, 134; farm crisis, effect of, 129; PERB, 144; tri-offer arbitration, 102–103, 116

Jacoby, Sanford M., 120
Joint Labor-Management Committee, 121

Kansas, 29, 33, 34, 52, 55–56, 59, 84–85, 88, 93, 96, 102, 137; grievance arbitration, 130, 134; impasse procedures, 104
Kennedy, John F., 37
Kochan, Thomas A., 114

Labor-management cooperation, 120–121
Ledyard Board of Education (Conn.), 97
Ligonier Valley School District (NYPERA), 137
Littleton Education Association v. Arapahoe County School District No. 6, 96
Local 66, Boston Teachers Union v. School Commission of Boston, 106

Macomb County Community College (Michigan), 97
Maine, 23
Majure Transport Co. v. NLRB, 96

Mallinckrodt Chemical Works, 69
Market system, 38
Marlborough Firefighters, Local 1714 (Mass.), 106, 109
Massachusetts, 25, 60, 73, 106, 109, 124; arbitration, 134; League of City and Towns, 121
McClimon, James, 144
McLaughlin v. Tilendis, 65, 66–67
McNeese v. Board of Education, 66
Mediation, 103–105, 113
Meet and confer requirement, 22, 135
Michigan, 52; arbitration, 103; Detroit, 86
Minnesota, 24, 34, 106, 137; arbitration, 134; Public Employment Relations Act, 129
Mironi, Mordecai, 123
Missouri, 87
Montana, 75, 79, 141
Moscow, Michael H., 47
Munzenrider, R., 78

Na-Mac Product Corp., 96
Nation v. State of Wyoming ex. rel. Fire Fighters Local 279, 97
National Academy of Arbitrators, 134
National Industrial Recovery Act, 52
National Labor Board, 52
National Labor Relations Act, 4, 11, 31, 33, 34, 59, 141–143; amended, 16–18; bargaining

issues, 28; bargaining unit determination, 69; enforcement, 53; good-faith bargaining, 82–83, 88–92, 127; grievance arbitration, 130; Landrum- Griffin amendments, 60–61 unfair labor practices, 75
National Labor Relations Board, 24, 59, 128; Office of the General Counsel, 53
National Union of Marine Cooks & Stewards v. NLRB, 96
Nevada, 30
New Deal, 52, 60
New Jersey, 84, 107; arbitration, 117
New York, 22, 33, 85, 115–116, 124; Constitution, 128; New York City, 86, 116; Taylor Act, 25, 34, 88–89
NLRB v. Atkins & Co., 78
NLRB v. Katz, 137
NLRB v. Norfolk Shipbuilding & Drydock Corp., 96
NLRB v. Truitt Manufacturing Co., 97
NLRB v. Wooster Division of Borg Warner Corp., 34, 96
North Carolina, 34

Ohio, 29, 30, 33, 108, 141; impasse procedures, 101–103
Oregon, 128, 137
Organization, employee, 64

Pegnetter, Richard, 116, 124
Pennsylvania, 68, 70–71, 74–75, 79, 137; grievance arbitration, 130

Perez v. Board of Public Commissioners of the City of Los Angeles, 66–67
Pontiac Police Officers Association v. City of Pontiac, 79
Providence Teachers Union Local 958 v. School Committee of Providence, 137
Public Employment Relations Board, 31
Public goods, 7, 43–46
Purdue University, 119

Railway Labor Act, 139
Representation, 23
Rhode Island, 23; impasse procedures, 104
Right-to-work law, 30, 93
Rockland Professional Fire Fighters Association v. City of Rockland, 138

Saginaw Township Board of Education (Michigan), 97
Salt Lake City v. International Association of Firefighters, 109
Scanlon Plan, 120
Scope of bargaining, 23, 28–29, 32, 81–84; effects, 84–86
Security, union, 30
Sergeant Bluff-Luton Community School District (Iowa), 97
Shelton v. Tucker, 65
Sloan v. Warren Civil Service Commission, 79
Smith, Adam, 38–40, 44
Smith v. Arkansas State Highway Employees, Local 1315, 66–67

Social Security Act, 14
South Carolina, University of, 119
South Dakota, 107
Southern Saddlery Co., 96
Sovereignty, 41–42, 46
Spielberg Manufacturing Co., 138
Spokane v. Spokane Police Guild, 109
State of New York v. AFSCME Council, 82, 137
Stern, James, 114
Stieber, Jack, 78
Strikes, 29, 32, 111–112, 117; alternative to, 100

Taylor, Benjamin, 52, 60
Taylor Committee, 115
Taxes, 76
Tenure, 16
Texas, 22, 34, 87
Textile Workers Union of America v. Lincoln Mills of Alabama, 130
Torrington v. Metal Product Workers Local 645, 138
Town of Stratford (Conn.), 137
Tripartite boards, 56

Tucker Act, 42

Unfair labor practices, 25–27, 74–75, 106
Uniform Arbitration Act, 144
United Steelworkers v. American Manufacturing, 131
United Steelworkers v. Enterprise Wheel & Car Corp., 131
United Steelworkers v. Warrior and Gulf Navigation Co., 131
U.S. Constitution, 63, 76; First amendment, 65–66, 93; Fourteenth amendment, 66
Utah, 107

Vaca v. Sipes, 138
Vermont State Employees Association v. State of Vermont, 97
Virginia, 34, 86
Virginia v. Arlington County, 96

Washington, 107; grievance arbitration, 130
West Virginia, 22
Wichita Public Schools Employees Union, Local 513 v. Smith, 135
Wisconsin, 37, 68, 78
Witney, Fred, 52, 60

ABOUT THE AUTHORS

DAVID A. DILTS is Professor of Labor Relations and Economics at Indiana University at Fort Wayne. He is also a member of the National Academy of Arbitrators. He has authored or co-authored over 60 articles concerning labor relations matters in journals such as *Management Science, Journal of Labor Research, Industrial Relations, Arbitration Journal, Labor Law Journal*, and *Journal of Collective Negotiations in the Public Sector*. He has co-authored six books concerning labor relations.

CLARENCE R. DEITSCH is Professor of Economics at Ball State University. Professor Deitsch is an arbitrator with nearly twenty years experience and serves as permanent arbitrator on the panels of the United States Postal Service. He has co-authored five books and over 30 articles in such journals as *Journal of Collective Negotiations in the Public Sector, Arbitration Journal, Journal of Labor Research*, and *Labor Law Journal*.

ALI RASSULI is Associate Professor of Economics and Chairman of the Department of Economics and Finance in the School of Business Management Sciences at Indiana University at Fort Wayne. Professor Rassuli has published extensively on labor relations and labor economics topics. His articles have appeared in journals such as *Journal of Post-Keynesian Economics, Toledo Law Review*, and *Journal of Collective Negotiations in the Public Sector*.